100 BEST
JEWISH RECIPES

100 BEST JEWISH RECIPES

MODERN CLASSICS, FROM EVERYDAY MEALS
TO FOOD FOR SPECIAL OCCASIONS

Evelyn
Rose

PAVILION

CONTENTS

FOREWORD

Every cook I know has their "go-to recipes" – a handful of tried, trusted and much-loved dishes that always work and never fail to delight. Fans of Evelyn Rose, the doyenne of Anglo-Jewish cooking for over half a century, are no exception. In virtually every copy of the classic **The New Complete International Jewish Cookbook** there are certain pages where these well-thumbed books naturally fall open to reveal the telltale signs of their owner's "greatest hits" ... a beetroot-pink stain beside Borscht on the Rocks, a trace of red wine in the margin of Florentine Beef Stew, or a buttery fingermark over the method for Lemon Cake.

This new volume represents one hundred of Evelyn Rose's own best-loved recipes. With over a thousand in **The New Complete** alone, choosing just one in ten was no mean feat, but this selection represents not only some of her personal favourites – as well as those of her fans – but her conviction that Jewish food is a living, evolving cuisine, rooted in tradition but inspired by the present, just as it has been for centuries.

For Evelyn, drawing inspiration from the tastes and ingredients of foreign lands, incorporating current thinking on health and nutrition, and using new technology to save time and effort are the keys to modern Jewish cooking and to securing its future with new generations of cooking enthusiasts.

The recipes in this new collection, from Syrian Cheese Puffs to Gefilte Fish Provençale, epitomize these principles in addition to Evelyn's eclectic and adventurous approach to bringing new flavours to the Jewish table. In fact, whenever she was asked for a definition of Jewish food, her answer was simple: "It's food that Jews eat," wherever they might live or hail from.

Whether the recipe's heritage is haimische, Sephardi, Mediterranean or Asian, my mother passionately believed that each dish must have *ta'am* – that extra something that makes it taste special, and so worth the effort for busy people to put on their table. She tested and fine-tuned each dish time and time again to ensure success for the home cook. This guarantee of fabulous food and recipes that "always work" is doubtless the reason why Evelyn's definitive work, **The Complete International Jewish Cookbook**, later revised by my mother and me, has been continuously in print since it was first published in 1976, and why her fans refer to it as their "bible".

When my mother wrote these recipes she also added her zest for life, a taste for adventure and her own unique qualities: devotion to her craft, commitment to her readers, and an extra ingredient of her own – a large helping of love, all made possible by the support of her companion, taste-taster and greatest fan of all, her husband, Myer. Within these pages, you will find all this – and more – in generous measure. Enjoy.

Judi Rose
London, 2015

INTRODUCTION

ORIGINS

You can almost pinpoint the exact occasion, in the second millennium BCE, when the art of Jewish cookery was born. On that day, the course of world history was changed when the matriarch Rebecca, by the judicious use of herbs and spices, gave the savour of wild venison to the insipid flesh of a young kid, and established a culinary philosophy of 'taste with economy' that has been followed by her descendants ever since.

When Rebecca made her kid casserole and her son Esau sold his birthright for a bowl of lentil soup, the everyday food of those early Jews was primitive in the extreme. Except on special occasions, the staple diet consisted of boiled vegetables – such as leeks, garlic and onions – and salads of raw herbs, with boiled meat cooked only on a holiday. During the following 2,000 years, the Jews became in turn the subjects of the four civilizations in which the art of the kitchen was first evolved. When the empires of the Egyptians, Persians, Greeks and Romans had faded into history, their cooking methods survived – in the kitchens of their former subjects.

To this day, Jewish households, during Pesach (the Feast of the Passover, see page 15), make a sweetmeat of dried apricots which their ancestors learned about when they were slaves in Egypt; they make a stuffed strudel with the same filling of poppy seeds and honey that was used to garnish the fattened dormice at Trimalchio's famous Roman feast; and during Shavuot (the Feast of Weeks, see page 15) they bake honey and cheese cakes that are a legacy of the many years of Seleucid rule.

If these 'remembrances of foods past' were the sum total of Jewish cooking, it is doubtful that it would have survived to the present day. Jewish tradition teaches that when Moses descended from Mount Sinai he gave the Jews the code of culinary practice by which they have conducted their kitchens ever since, and which has been responsible, to a large extent, for the unique flavour and character of their food.

In the Jewish dietary laws, there are prohibitions: no shellfish; no pig; no carrion; no birds of prey; no thing that crawls upon its belly. Then there are the categories of permitted foods: only those fish that have fins and scales; only those beasts that chew the cud and have cloven hooves; only those birds that have been slaughtered according to the Law. Then there are the cooking and serving instructions for these permitted foods: foods of animal and dairy origin not to

be combined either during the cooking or the serving; dairy foods to be served after meat foods only when a specified number of hours has elapsed; meat to be purged of its blood before use.

However, it was in the Ten Commandments themselves that there appeared those instructions which have resulted in the development of some of the most typical of Jewish foods – those dishes that can be cooked one day and served the next. 'On the seventh day thou shalt do no work, neither thy maidservant nor thy manservant,' said the Law, and so all day Thursday, and most of Friday before dusk would be spent making salads, liver pâté, soups, fruit pies, yeast cakes and, in particular, those meat and vegetable casseroles that could be left in a low oven overnight, such as Cholent and Tsimmes.

The need to differentiate between meat and milk meals encouraged the development of many delicious dairy dishes made from velvety kaese, a soft cheese made from naturally soured milk. These dishes include cheese kreplach (a form of ravioli), lokshen and kaese (noodle and cheese casserole), and the blintze, a paper-thin pancake stuffed with slightly sweetened cream cheese, which is the most famous Jewish dish to be absorbed into international cuisine.

The shortage of kosher meat in the ghettos of medieval Europe forced households to find ways of stretching their meagre supply. Usually, meat would be minced and used as a stuffing for a variety of different doughs and vegetables.

Those Jews who lived in the Middle East stuffed carrots, aubergines, tomatoes and even leeks, using an ingenious metal 'excavator' to remove the vegetable flesh from the skin. When meat became more plentiful, other methods of cooking it were adopted, but all were based on braising or casseroling, for kosher meat is used only a few days after it has been killed and tends to be tough when it is dry-roasted.

Some of the most interesting Jewish foods are those cooked in celebration of a festival (see pages 12–15). In biblical times, these festivals were the occasions for the family to make a pilgrimage on foot to the Temple at Jerusalem, where they would offer the first ripe fruits from their fields, as well as bread and cakes made from the new season's wheat.

No artificial leavening may be used in Pesach baking, so whisked sponges and meringues are the most popular confectionery. As ordinary flour may not be used, and so ground nuts, matzah meal and potato starch are substituted. There are almond macaroons, whisked sponges and ground-nut torten, and cinnamon balls made of ground almonds and sugar; many of these are made from recipes dating back to the Middle Ages.

Perhaps the finest Jewish cooks of Western Europe were those who lived in the old Austro-Hungarian Empire. To these women, Friday was 'strudel day'; they would rise at 6 a.m. to stretch the tissue-paper-thin dough on to a cloth laid on the kitchen table and then make metre-wide tins of yeast cake, topped with cherries (kirschen kuchen), plums (zwetschen kuchen) or cheese (kaese kuchen), which would last the family until after the Sabbath on the following day.

The cooking that is done in the majority of Western Jewish households, however, owes much of its inspiration to the fish and fowl of Poland, the Czech Republic, Slovakia and the states that border the Baltic Sea. In the freshwater lakes of these countries swam the carp and the bream that were used to make the famous gefilte fish. Today, Western Jews use haddock, hake, cod and halibut to make this delicious fish dish, which has a close affinity to the *quenelles de brochet* of France. If you visit Israel, you will have this mixture served in a pepper and tomato sauce, or as a starter, formed into little balls that are fried and served with pickled cucumbers. Gefilte fish apart, the new generations of Israeli Jews have discarded many of the traditional dishes of those families who came from the colder lands of Europe, and now enjoy a far lighter diet of vegetables, dairy foods and fish, albeit spiced with many traditional dishes of the Middle East.

Food of an entirely different nature from that prepared by Western Jews is cooked by those Jews who were expelled from Spain by Ferdinand and Isabella in 1492 and settled in many of the countries bordering the Mediterranean. The cookery of the Sephardim, as they are known, is spicy and aromatic, and their cakes, flavoured with rosewater and almond oil, seem to have come straight out of the Arabian Nights.

THE RECIPES

Jewish food is no stranger to innovation – how else could it have survived as a recognizable cuisine through so many vicissitudes of fortune? The dishes in this book have come from a wide variety of Jewish communities across the globe. Some are traditional in the sense that they have been passed down through several generations. Others, however, are even now being absorbed into Jewish food culture. This enrichment of our cuisine has been going on for centuries and is one reason for its survival. The recipes in this book reflect the excitement, the variety, the flavour, the history and the love that is interwoven in what we call 'Jewish food', and I hope that it will in some small way help to preserve it for generations to come.

FESTIVALS AND FOOD

The Jewish year follows the Lunar calendar, so the date of each festival in the Western (Gregorian) calendar varies from year to year.

ROSH HASHANAH
NEW YEAR
1 and 2 Tishri
(September/October)

Ever since the return from Babylon, where the art of sugar cookery is thought to have originated, Jewish households have made all kinds of sweet foods at this festival as a symbol of the sweetness they hope for in the year ahead. This sweetness is often introduced into dishes by using dried fruits or honey. While all kinds of fruit are served at Rosh Hashanah, the apple is the symbolic fruit of the season, expressing in both its sweetness and its round shape the hope for a satisfying and sweet New Year. As at every other festival, no Rosh Hashanah is complete without a platter of fried gefilte fish (see page 94).

YOM KIPPUR
THE DAY OF ATONEMENT
10 Tishri
(September/October)

At Yom Kippur, the Jewish people seek to atone for the sins between themselves and God. Although it is a Fast Day, the main preparations for the cook are concerned with making two special meals – that before the Fast on Kol Nidre (the eve of Yom Kippur), and that eaten 25 hours later, when it has ended. Simple, soothing food that is satisfying without being thirst-making is essential for Kol Nidre night. Chicken soup with kreplach or matzah balls, followed by an uncomplicated roast or braised bird, and a fruity dessert, followed by a large glass of lemon tea, is the general Ashkenazi pattern. After the Fast in Ashkenazi households, there are only minor variations from the sequence of the meal: a glass of Kiddush wine, then a piece of buttered kuchen or plain cake, with several cups of tea and some kind of smoked or pickled fish – some say it's to restore mineral salts lost by the body during the day, but most people enjoy the way a spiced food tickles the fasting palate – and then to the table for a fish meal and a not-too-demanding dessert.

SUKKOT
THE FEAST OF TABERNACLES
15 Tishri
(September/October)

Sukkot, the week-long autumn harvest festival commemorating the years that the Jews had to wander in the wilderness, living out their days in makeshift huts, is a particularly happy occasion in the Jewish calendar. Many families make their own Sukkah, or Tabernacle, where they eat their meals, and every house is sweet with the fragrance of fruit and flowers. Immediately after the end of the Yom Kippur Fast, it is the custom in many communities for the men to construct a Sukkah in the grounds of the synagogue, then line its roof – which must be partly open to the sky – with greenery. It is then decorated with fruit and vegetables – these are usually sent to hospitals and old people's homes at the end of the festival. At the end of each service, the congregation moves into the Sukkah for Kiddush (benediction) and a slice of a traditional cake or biscuit. To symbolize the richness of the harvest, stuffed foods of all kinds are served as both savouries and sweets. Cabbages, vine leaves, tomatoes, aubergines and peppers are stuffed with lean minced beef and braised in a sweet-and-sour tomato or meat sauce. Known as holishkes and gevikelte kraut, these are the most popular in the West, but in Israel stuffed aubergines (chatzilim) are making a new tradition.

SIMCHAT TORAH
THE REJOICING
OF THE LAW
23 Tishri
(September/October)

The festival of Simchat Torah is the moment when the last portion of the Torah (the Five Books of Moses) is read in the synagogue, and the weekly readings from the Sefer Torah (the Scroll of the Law) start all over again with a passage from Beresheit (Genesis). It concludes the month of High Holy Days (September and October in the Western calendar). On Simchat Torah, all the Scrolls of the Law are taken from the Holy Ark – the holiest place in the synagogue in which they are stored – and paraded round the synagogue with much singing and dancing, in which the whole congregation joins. Children take advantage of the lack of the usual decorum to wave flags and pelt the readers with sweets – which they immediately scramble to pick up. A special reception is held after the service either to honour the two 'Bridegrooms of the Law', who have read the final and first portions of the Law, or just the Chatan Torah, while the other – the Chatan Beresheit – is honoured on the following Saturday on Shabbat Beresheit. Either way, everyone enjoys delicious vegetable dips and luscious cakes.

CHANUKKAH
THE FEAST OF LIGHTS
25 Kislev
(December)

The famous defeat of the Greeks in the second century BCE by Judas Maccabaeus (in Hebrew, Yehuda HaMaccabee) and his followers is celebrated during the eight days of Chanukkah with parties and presents – particularly for children.

Tradition states that after Yehuda's family, the Hasmoneans, had been inspired by their father, Mattathias the High Priest, to defeat the tyrant Antiochus IV – who had desecrated the Temple in Jerusalem with pagan rites – there was only enough pure, undefiled oil for the sacred Menorah (seven-branched candelabra) for it to burn for 24 hours. By a miracle, the Menorah stayed alight for eight days and nights until more pure oil could be obtained.

So in every Jewish home, an extra candle is lit in the Chanukkah (the eight-branched candelabra) on each of the eight nights of Chanukkah, and the family and their friends gather round to sing the famous hymn of praise, 'Maoz Tsur' ('Rock of Ages') as they celebrate the Miracle of the Oil. So it's not surprising that foods cooked in oil have become traditional at this festival, as well as rich and sweet foods such as trifles and fruit cakes.

PURIM
THE FEAST OF LOTS
14 Adar
(February/March)

Purim occurs exactly one month before Passover. It commemorates the downfall of Haman, the evil vizier of King Ahasuerus (Artaxerxes II), who in the fifth century BCE formulated his own Final Solution by planning the massacre of the entire Jewish population of Persia. According to the story, Haman drew lots to decide on which day to exterminate the Jews. However, he ended up on the gallows he had prepared for his enemies, and his notoriety is perpetuated in a variety of cakes and sweetmeats.

PESACH
PASSOVER
15 Nissan
(March/April)

Each spring, Passover, the great festival of freedom commemorates the liberation of the Jews from slavery in Egypt more than 3,500 years ago. This festival is seen as a time of renewal, a great family occasion, when everyone gathers to enjoy the Seder – the ceremonial meal. The order of the courses is laid down in the Haggadah, a text used by Jewry worldwide for centuries past. During the Seder meal, the story of the Exodus from Egypt is read from the Haggadah, and a succession of symbolic foods, displayed on a special plate, are tasted by everyone at the table. The kitchen is filled with the wonderful perfume of eingemacht (Passover preserves) and lemon curd, and the cakes and biscuits – the macaroons, sponge cakes and cinnamon balls, whose recipes have been passed down the chain from mother to daughter since early medieval times – are ready and waiting for the family's verdict.

SHAVUOT
PENTECOST OR THE FEAST OF WEEKS
6 Sivan
(May/June)

In earlier days, when the Temple still stood in Jerusalem, Shavuot was celebrated as a great agricultural festival, when the start of the wheat harvest was marked by offerings of newly baked bread. Every man brought the first fruits of his crops to the Temple, while his wife ground flour from the new season's wheat and baked special cakes and bread in honour of the occasion. Today Jewish people commemorate those early days by decorating the house with flowers and plants and by taking them as gifts to the synagogue. This festival also celebrates the giving of the Torah – the code of Jewish Law – to Moses on Mount Sinai. In the Torah are set out the dietary laws – the regulations that relate to the preparation and consumption of food in the community. Another tradition links the custom to the gift of the land 'flowing with milk and honey'. So milk and foods derived from it have become the most famous symbolic foods of this festival.

These dairy ingredients are made into some of the most delicious dishes of Jewish cuisine – such as the cheesecakes and blintzes, and the kreplach and lokshen casseroles.

SMALL PLATES

CHATZILIM
'POOR MAN'S CAVIARE'

SERVES 4–6 AS A STARTER, 8–10 AS A DIP
KEEPS FOR 2 WEEKS IN THE FRIDGE | DO NOT FREEZE

A delicious eastern Mediterranean starter, particularly popular in Israel, chatzilim is served like a pâté with pitta or toast and butter, or as a stuffing for tomatoes. It is also known as *Potljelly* by Romanian Jews.

450g/1 lb aubergines

1 garlic clove, crushed

1 tbsp finely chopped onion

juice of ½ lemon

1 tbsp extra virgin olive oil

1 tsp sea salt

10 grinds of black pepper

1 tbsp finely chopped parsley

1 tbsp finely chopped green pepper (optional)

black olives and pitta or challah (see page 140), to serve

Cut off the prickly stalk-ends of the aubergines, then prick all over with a fork – this prevents them bursting. Traditionally the aubergines are grilled over charcoal, giving the dish its characteristic smoky flavour. However, unless you have a charcoal grill to hand it's much more convenient to preheat the oven to 230°C/450°F/Gas 8 and bake them 8–30 minutes until they have begun to collapse and a skewer meets no resistance when the centre is pierced.

If more convenient, lay them on a paper towel and cook in the microwave until tender. Leave to stand for 1 minute, then pierce with a skewer to test as before. If you want a smoky flavour, char each softened aubergine by holding it briefly over the open flame of a gas stove (use barbecue tongs or a long-handled fork). Allow to cool for a few minutes, then cut into half and scoop out the flesh from the skin.

Chop the remaining ingredients into it using a large cook's knife, mezzaluna or hackmesser (an old-fashioned wooden-handled chopper), adding the olive oil and lemon juice last. Taste and add more lemon juice and seasonings, if necessary.

Put into a shallow pottery dish. Garnish with black olives and serve with challah or warm pitta bread.

HUMMUS B'TAHINA
WITH TOASTED PINE NUTS

SERVES 4–6, OR 15 WITH 2 OTHER DIPS
KEEPS FOR 3 DAYS IN THE FRIDGE | DO NOT FREEZE

1 small bunch of flat-leaf parsley

2 tbsp extra virgin olive oil

200g/7oz good-quality ready-made hummus

1½ tbsp tahina

1 tbsp lemon juice

½ tsp ground cumin

2 tbsp pine nuts, toasted in a dry pan

Process the parsley with the oil in the food processor until the oil is bright green and the parsley finely chopped. Put in a small bowl and reserve.

Process all the other ingredients except the pine nuts until evenly blended. Taste for seasoning, adding extra lemon juice if not tangy enough. Spoon into a fairly shallow dish. Just before serving, drizzle with the herbed oil and sprinkle with the pine nuts.

LIPTAUER CHEESE

SUFFICIENT TO TOP 60 SAVOURY CRACKERS OR SLICES OF FRENCH BREAD
KEEPS FOR 1 WEEK IN THE FRIDGE | DO NOT FREEZE

This Viennese cream cheese dip has a deliciously piquant mix of flavours.

200g/7oz low-fat soft cheese

1 tsp anchovy paste, or 2 finely chopped canned anchovies

2 tsp capers, rinsed and drained

1 tsp Dijon or English mustard

2 tsp paprika

a few twists of black pepper

celery salt (optional)

1 tbsp snipped chives

Beat all the ingredients together, then leave for several hours to develop the flavour.

CHEESE BLINTZES

SERVES 6 AS A STARTER
**FILLED BUT UNBROWNED BLINTZES KEEP FOR 1 DAY IN THE FRIDGE | UNFILLED PANCAKES FREEZE FOR
3 MONTHS, FILLED PANCAKES FREEZE FOR 1 MONTH**

These are one of the glories of Jewish cuisine. The Yiddish word for these paper-thin pancakes is *bletlach* – or *skeleton* leaves – which gives some indication of how thin they should be.

FOR THE BATTER

125g/4oz plain flour

1 pinch of salt

2 large eggs

2 tsp oil

125ml/4fl oz milk

125ml/4fl oz water

butter and oil, for frying

FOR THE FILLING

350g/12oz curd cheese, or sieved cottage cheese, mixed with 2 tbsp soured cream, yogurt or fromage frais or 1 egg yolk (whichever is most convenient)

1 tsp sugar

1 pinch of salt

TO SERVE

ice-cold soured cream

Sift the flour and salt into a bowl. Make a well, drop in the eggs and oil and stir. Gradually add the milk and water until smooth. Beat with a whisk until the surface is covered with tiny bubbles. Leave the batter to rest for half an hour. To make the filling, mix all the ingredients together and leave until required.

Stir the batter well and pour into a jug – it should be the consistency of single cream. Put a 16–18cm/6–7in diameter non-stick omelette pan over a medium heat for 3 minutes, then drop in a teaspoonful of oil, and swirl it round the base and side of the pan. Wipe out any excess with a paper towel. Using a pad of paper towel, smear the entire inner surface of the pan very thinly with butter, then pour in a thick layer of batter, swirling it round so that it covers the side and base of the pan. The heat will immediately set a thin layer so that the excess can be poured back into the jug. The blintze should be so thin that by the time the sides begin to curl from the pan, the bottom will be brown and the top side dry. Turn the blintze out on to a sheet of greaseproof paper. Repeat the process until all the pancakes have been made. Stack the pancakes on top of each other, browned-side up.

To stuff, place a pancake brown-side up on the work surface. Spread a tablespoon of the filling thinly over the bottom half, turn in the sides and roll up into a long thin roll. Repeat with each pancake. Heat 4 tbsp butter and 2 teaspoons of oil in a wide frying pan. The moment the butter stops foaming, put in the stuffed blintzes, join-side upwards. Cook gently for 3 minutes until golden brown, turn and cook the second side. Serve with soured cream.

CHICKEN LIVER PÂTÉ
JEWISH STYLE

SERVES 6 AS A STARTER, 8–10 AS A SPREAD
KEEPS FOR 5 DAYS IN THE FRIDGE | FREEZES FOR 1 MONTH

The onion in this recipe is sautéed to caramelize it and enrich the flavour of this superb pâté. Using cooked rather than raw onion also helps the pâté keep for longer. This kind of liver pâté can be made with a mincer, but to get a smooth and 'creamy' texture it should be made in a food processor.

3 eggs (1 for the garnish)

1 onion, finely chopped

1 garlic clove, crushed

50g/2oz margarine or 4 tbsp rendered chicken fat or chicken-flavoured vegetable fat

5–10 grinds of sea salt

350g/12oz ready-koshered chicken livers

15 grinds of black pepper

1 good pinch of freshly grated nutmeg

TO SERVE

warm French bread, crackers or slices of challah (see page 140)

Hard-boil the eggs for 10 minutes, drain, then return to the pan, cover with cold water and then leave in the pan.

Fry the onion and the garlic gently in the fat until very soft and a rich brown (this is important if the right depth of flavour is to be achieved). As the onion cooks, sprinkle it with the sea salt.

Shell the eggs and cut in half. Put 1 egg aside.

Put the onion and garlic with their cooking juices into the food processor and process until smooth, then add 2 eggs and all the remaining ingredients and process again until smooth. Taste and add more seasonings if necessary, but remember that the flavours will intensify over the next few hours.

Turn into a terrine, oval gratin dish or divide between individual cocottes. Chill, covered with cling film, preferably overnight. Refrigerate the extra egg.

One hour before serving, remove the pâté from the fridge and leave at room temperature. Just before serving, pass the remaining egg through a food mill or sieve and use it to decorate the top of the pâté. Serve with warm French bread, crackers or slices of challah.

EGG AND SPRING ONION FORSPEISE

SERVES 6 AS A STARTER, 15 AS A SPREAD
KEEPS FOR 1 DAY IN THE FRIDGE | DO NOT FREEZE

This delicious starter is traditionally made with a hackmesser, or wooden-handled chopper. In many families, this long and tedious job was performed by one of the men, using a hackbrettle – a wooden chopping board with sides. A mincer produces entirely the wrong texture, but it can be made just as effectively with a food processor.

1 bunch of spring onions, plus 10cm/4in of the green, or 1 onion, cut into 2.5cm/1in chunks

8 hard-boiled eggs, shelled and halved

4 rounded tbsp soft margarine or rendered chicken fat or chicken-flavoured vegetable fat

½ tsp salt

10 grinds of black pepper

TO SERVE

warm French bread, crackers or slices of challah (see page 140)

Put the onions into the bowl of the food processor and pulse for 3 seconds until roughly chopped. Add all the remaining ingredients and pulse for a further 5 seconds until finely chopped and blended.

Turn into a small gratin dish, smooth the top level and mark with a pattern using the blade of a knife. Cover and chill for at least an hour before serving.

Serve with warm French bread, crackers or slices of challah.

VARIATION
For a dairy meal, soft butter can be used instead of the other fats.

OLD-FASHIONED PICKLED HERRINGS

SERVES 6 | PICTURED ON PAGE 24
KEEPS FOR 6 WEEKS IN THE FRIDGE, BUT BECOMES MORE ACIDIC IN TIME

Sometimes called 'Bismarcks' or 'rollmops', these can be bought in jars, but they are especially delicious if you make your own. If salt herrings are not available, soak 6 fresh cleaned and boned herrings in 50g/2oz salt and 575ml/1 pint water for 2 hours, then continue as below.

3 salt herrings

white pepper

1 onion, thinly sliced

1 large unpeeled lemon, sliced

1 tbsp pickling spice

2 bay leaves

1 dried chilli pepper

575ml/1 pint white vinegar

2½ tbsp brown sugar

Behead the herrings, slit the belly and remove the entrails. Put the fish in a glass casserole dish (so that the smell will not linger) and place under the cold-water tap. Leave the water running in a gentle trickle. After 15 minutes, turn off the tap and let the herrings stand overnight covered in cold water.

Next day, lift the fish out of the water and drain well. Lay them on a piece of newspaper or kitchen paper, hold the tail firmly and scrape from the tail to the head with a blunt knife to remove loose scales. Wash again in cold water and put on a board. Open the front, turn the fish over and press the back with the flat of the hand. Turn over again and the backbone will lift out easily. Remove the tails if you prefer, and any other loose bones.

Sprinkle each herring very lightly with white pepper, add 2–3 thin rings of onion, then roll up from tail to head. If the herrings are large, you may find it easier to split them lengthways before rolling. Skewer them closed with wooden cocktail sticks. Put in a glass jar in alternate layers with the lemon, onion and spices.

Put the vinegar and sugar into a pan and bring to the boil, then immediately turn off the heat and leave until it is lukewarm. Pour over the herrings. Cover and refrigerate for 4 days before using.

Serve in 1.25cm/½in slices, either speared on a cocktail stick or as an hors d'oeuvre garnished with the pickled onion slices.

HAIMISCHE PICKLED CUCUMBERS

MAKES 5KG/10LB | PICTURED ON PAGE 25
KEEPS FOR 4–6 WEEKS IN THE FRIDGE

Pickled cucumbers are known as *ugekes* in Yiddish, and this recipe is the most delicious version of the pickle that I know – it originates from Lithuania and the name *haimische* means comfort food. The cucumbers are usually pickled a month before Rosh Hashana (New Year), so that they provide a special, homely treat for the holiday.

2l/4 pints water

100g/4oz coarse or kosher salt

1kg/2¼lb firm green gherkins or ridge cucumbers 10–15cm/ 4–6 in long

FOR THE SPICES

1 piece of dried root ginger

2 red pickling chillies

2 garlic cloves

1 tbsp mixed pickling spice

2 bay leaves

1 tbsp distilled malt vinegar

Put the water into a large pan with the salt and spices. Bring to the boil, stirring until the salt has dissolved. Boil rapidly for 5 minutes. Take off the heat and leave until absolutely cold.

Scrub the cucumbers thoroughly with a small soft-bristle nailbrush (kept especially for the purpose), discarding any that have soft or damaged parts. Rinse them in cold water, then layer in a large bowl. As each layer is put in the bowl, scatter over some of the spices strained from the liquid.

Cover the cucumbers with a large, upturned plate, then weigh down with something heavy, such as a couple of full tins wrapped in a plastic bag. Pour the cold pickling solution down the side of the bowl until it covers the plate to a depth of 2.5cm/1 in. Cover with a muslin cloth or thin tea towel and leave in a very cool place for 10 days.

After 10 days, skim the froth off the surface. If any bluish mould has appeared, remove that too. Cover again and leave for a further week.

Skim again, and test by slicing into a cucumber. If the taste is not right – it should be salty and slightly sour – leave them for a further week, or until ready.

Skim again, pack into large sterilized glass containers and fill up with the pickling liquid until the cucumbers are completely submerged. Store in the fridge.

SYRIAN CHEESE PUFFS

MAKES ABOUT 25 CHEESE PUFFS
MAKE AND BAKE THE SAME DAY | DO NOT REHEAT

Since the separation of meat and milk foods laid down in the dietary laws, Jewish cooking has always put special emphasis on dairy dishes. Indeed, Jewish dairy specialities, such as cheese blintzes (see page 21), are now eaten in general as well as the Jewish community. These delicious little bites, also known as savoury Sephardi cheesecakes, can be served as a main course for a dairy lunch or with drinks. They are always a hit at parties.

200g/7oz mature or extra-mature Cheddar cheese

1 large egg

½ tsp salt, less if the cheese is salty

500g/1lb 2oz puff pastry

2 tbsp sesame seeds

Cut the cheese into pieces that will fit into the feed tube of your food processor, then wrap in cling film and freeze for 1 hour – this stops the cheese from melting and gumming up the mechanism when you grate it. Grate the cheese using the fine grater disc, then put in a large bowl.

Preheat the oven to 220°C/425°F/Gas 7 and line two large baking trays with baking parchment. Whisk the egg to blend (reserve 1 tablespoon for glazing the puffs). Add the egg and the salt to the cheese and mix to a sticky paste.

Roll the pastry to the thickness of a knife blade, then cut with 6cm/2½in plain cutters into about 25 rounds. Alternatively, cut into 6cm/2½in squares.

Dampen the edges of each piece, place a teaspoon of filling in the centre and fold over to form a half moon (or triangle if you are starting with squares). Seal firmly with the tines of a fork. Arrange on the prepared baking trays. Brush with the beaten egg, then dip the brushed side in a bowl of sesame seeds to coat. Bake for 10–15 minutes until crisp and golden. Serve warm.

COCKTAIL FISH BALLS

SERVES 4–6 (MAKES 30 SMALL BALLS)
KEEP FOR 1 DAY IN THE FRIDGE | FREEZE FOR 3 MONTHS

FOR THE FISH MIX

500g/1lb 2oz fish
(a mixture of haddock and cod)

½ onion

1 large egg

1 tsp salt, plus extra to salt the fish

5 grinds of black pepper

1 tsp sugar

1 tbsp oil

30g/1oz medium matzah meal, plus extra if needed

FOR THE COATING

60g/2oz medium matzah meal

oil for deep-frying

Wash and salt the fish and leave to drain. Put the onion into the food processor, together with the egg, seasoning and oil, then process to a smooth purée. Pour this purée into a large bowl and stir in the matzah meal, then leave to swell.

Working in batches, process the fish in the processor for 5 seconds until finely chopped, then add to the onion purée and blend in using a large fork. Repeat until all the fish has been processed, then mix thoroughly. The mixture should be firm enough to shape into a soft ball. If it feels too 'cloggy', add 1 or 2 tablespoons of water and stir. If it feels very soft, stir in 1 or 2 extra tablespoons of matzah meal. Leave for half an hour, or overnight in the fridge. The fish mix is now ready to shape.

Use a very small spring-loaded ice cream scoop to portion out the mixture, or partially fill a large vegetable piping bag without a nozzle, then pipe out in blobs the size of a walnut. Roll into little balls.

Put half the balls at a time into a large plastic bag containing the remaining matzah meal. Shake until the balls are evenly coated. Fry in deep, hot oil, at 180°C/360°F, or hot enough to brown a 2.5cm/1in cube of bread in 40 seconds. Fry quickly until golden brown, then drain on crumpled paper towels or a cooling rack set over a baking tray. Repeat until all the balls are fried, then leave to cool.

When the balls are quite cold, put into plastic bags and freeze until required. To serve, spread the frozen balls on to an oven tray and heat at 180°C/350°F/Gas 4 until crisp to the touch – about 5 minutes. Serve warm or cold speared on cocktail sticks with chrane (horseradish and beetroot relish) or Tartare Sauce (see page 180).

SOUPS

TRADITIONAL CHICKEN SOUP

SERVES 4–6

KEEPS FOR 3 DAYS IN THE FRIDGE | FREEZES FOR 3 MONTHS

Chicken soup is traditionally made by simmering a fowl with giblets in water flavoured with a variety of vegetables. However, if the fowl is to be casseroled rather than boiled for another dish, or a younger bird roasted or fried, then the soup can be made with just the wings and giblets with vegetables, and the flavour strengthened using a chicken stock cube.

1 whole or half chicken or fowl, plus wings and giblets (excluding livers)

2 tsp salt

1 pinch of white pepper

1 large onion

2 large carrots

leaves and top 5cm/2in of 2 celery stalks

1 sprig of parsley

1 very ripe tomato

TO SERVE

knaidlach (soup dumplings, see page 178) or lokshen, vermicelli or egg noodles

Put the bird, wings and giblets in a large, heavy soup pan with 1.75l/ 3 pints water, the salt and pepper (the feet would traditionally be added at this stage too). Cover and bring to the boil. Remove any froth with a large, wet metal spoon.

Peel the onion and carrots, cut in half and add to the pan with celery, parsley, and tomato. Bring back to the boil, then reduce the heat so that the liquid is barely bubbling. Cover and continue to simmer for a further 3 hours, either on top of the stove or in a slow oven at 150°C /300°F/Gas 2, or until the chicken feels very tender when a leg is prodded.

Strain the soup into a large bowl; reserve the giblets and carrots in another container. Pour off the fat in batches using a large fat separator. Alternatively, cover and put in the fridge overnight. Next day, remove any congealed fat and return the soup to the pan. (If there is a thick layer of fat, it can be heated in a pan to drive off any liquid and then, when it has stopped bubbling, cooled and stored like rendered raw fat.)

Cut the cooked giblets and the carrots into small dice. Add to the soup with the knaidlach, lokshen, vermicelli or egg noodles (allow approximately 15g/½oz per person of lokshen cooked according to packet directions). Reheat gently before serving.

CHICKEN SOUP – 3 WAYS

ALL RECIPES SERVE 4
KEEP FOR 3 DAYS IN THE FRIDGE | FREEZE FOR 3 MONTHS

The basis of these three soups is a completely defatted chicken stock with a selection of diced vegetables and a little optional vermicelli. Although ideal for slimmers, they are delicious enough to serve to non-dieters as well.

To defat the chicken stock quickly and completely, partly freeze it for 2–3 hours until the fat is solid enough to scrape off with a spoon. If you like a thicker soup, you may prefer the courgette and lettuce version opposite. All three soups will improve if left for at least 6 hours before serving. Reheat gently until bubbling.

CHICKEN NOODLE SOUP

1.2l/2 pints home-made (see page 176), or best-quality bought chicken stock

75g/3oz white part of a leek, diced

75g/3oz carrots, shredded

75g/3oz yellow pepper, deseeded and shredded

1 ring uncooked vermicelli pasta

2 tsp chopped parsley

salt and ground black pepper

Bring the stock to the boil, add the diced vegetables and the vermicelli, cover and simmer for 10 minutes. Taste and add salt and pepper if necessary. Add the parsley before serving.

CHICKEN, COURGETTE AND LETTUCE SOUP

680g/1 1/2lb courgettes, thinly sliced

1 tbsp minced dried onion (optional)

1.2l/2 pints home-made (see page 176) or best-quality bought chicken stock

1/2 tsp salt

15 grinds of black pepper

1 lettuce, shredded

2 tsp chopped parsley or snipped chives

Put the thinly sliced, unpeeled courgettes, onion (if using), stock, salt and pepper into a soup pan and simmer, covered, until the courgettes are soft – 10–15 minutes. Add the shredded lettuce and let the soup bubble, uncovered, for 3 minutes. Blend or process until smooth. Just before serving, stir in the parsley or chives.

CHICKEN, MUSHROOM AND COURGETTE SOUP

1.2l/2 pints home-made (see page 176)or best-quality bought chicken stock

125g/4 1/2oz very fresh mushrooms with stalks, wiped with a damp cloth, then thinly sliced

1 large carrot, cut into 1cm/1/2in cubes

1 courgette, cut into 1cm/1/2in slices

2 tsp tomato purée

2 tsp chopped parsley

salt and ground black pepper

Bring the stock to the boil, add the diced mushrooms, carrot and courgette. Stir in the tomato purée, then cover and simmer for 10 minutes. Taste and add salt and pepper if necessary. Add the parsley just before serving.

MOTHER'S MILCHIKE SOUP

SERVES 6
KEEPS FOR 3 DAYS IN THE FRIDGE | FREEZES FOR 3 MONTHS

This soup was made to herald summer in the villages of the Pale of Settlement, in Russia. It is fresh and simple, with the flavour of young vegetables. Some families make tiny knaidlach (see page 178), made with butter instead of chicken fat, and serve them in this soup.

3 tbsp butter

1 onion, finely chopped

4 new potatoes, cubed

1 carrot, grated

450g/1lb pack of fresh or frozen mixed special vegetables (including baby carrots and petit pois)

850ml/1½ pints water

1 tsp salt

1 pinch of black pepper

1 tsp sugar

1 tbsp cornflour

275ml/10fl oz milk

1 tbsp snipped chives or spring onion tops

Melt the butter in a heavy pan and 'sweat' the onion in the covered pan until soft and golden. Add the potatoes, carrot and mixed vegetables. Cover with the water, add the salt, pepper and sugar. Simmer, covered, for 30 minutes, or until all the vegetables are tender.

Mix the cornflour into the milk, then stir it into the soup and simmer, still stirring, for 3 minutes. Stir in the chives or spring onion tops.

HOBENE GROPEN
BEEF WITH PINHEAD OATMEAL SOUP

SERVES 4
KEEPS FOR 3 DAYS IN THE FRIDGE | FREEZES FOR 3 MONTHS

This is a creamy-textured soup that is especially rich in the B vitamins. It is made with a type of oats known in Jewish households as *hobene gropen* or *hubergrits*, but also called pinhead oatmeal. Because it is a wholegrain cereal, it does need to be simmered for several hours, but the result is a wonderfully sustaining winter soup.

3 tbsp hobene gropen (pinhead oatmeal)

225g/8oz or more shin of beef

1 tsp salt

½ tsp white pepper

1L/1¾ pints meat stock (see page 177)

1 large potato

1 onion

1 carrot

1 fat celery stalk

1 good sprig of parsley, plus extra chopped parsley, to serve

Put the hobene gropen into a small bowl, cover with boiling water. Leave to settle while you add the beef, with the salt and pepper, to the stock. Bring to the boil and skim off any froth with a metal spoon. Add the strained hobene gropen, reduce the heat so that the soup is barely bubbling, then cover and simmer in this way for 1 hour.

Meanwhile, cut the potato into 1.25cm/½in cubes, and dice the onion, carrot and celery into 5mm/¼in cubes. Add these vegetables to the soup, together with the parsley sprig. Cover again and simmer for a further 2 hours, by which time the soup should be creamy and the meat tender. Remove the sprig of parsley, taste the soup, and add more salt and pepper if required. Sprinkle with chopped parsley and serve piping hot.

To serve on the second day, add half a cup of water and reheat gently.

HAIMISCHE WINTER SOUP

SERVES 4
KEEPS FOR 3 DAYS IN THE FRIDGE | FREEZES FOR 3 MONTHS

Haimische can be roughly translated as comfort food, so this is *par excellence* the soup 'like Mama used to make'. Indeed, for nineteenth-century Russian and Polish peasants it was also their main dish of the day, as the pulses and cereals it contained made it extremely nourishing, while still cheap. The consistency of the soup can also be easily adjusted by boiling it down or diluting it with extra stock.

100g/4oz green split peas

60g/2¼oz red lentils

2 tbsp pearl barley

3 tbsp dried haricot beans

225g/8oz soup meat such as shin of beef (optional)

1L/1¾ pints home-made stock (see page 176), or 1.75L/3 pints water and 1 soup bone

1 tsp salt

5 grinds of black pepper

1 tsp fines herbes

1 large carrots, cut into 1cm/⅜in dice

1 celery stalk, cut into 2cm/¾in dice

white part of a fat leek, well washed and thinly sliced

1 large sprig of parsley

1 large carrot, coarsely grated

The day before making the soup, put the split peas, lentils, barley and haricot beans into a large bowl, cover with twice their depth of cold water and leave to soak and swell overnight.

Next day, put the meat and the stock (or the water and bone) with the salt into a large soup pan and bring to the boil. Skim off any froth with a wet metal spoon. Tip the cereals into a fine sieve to remove any excess soaking water, then put under the cold tap and rinse thoroughly until the water that drains from them is quite clear.

Add to the soup pan with the seasonings and all the vegetables except the grated carrot. Bring back to the boil, then reduce the heat until the mixture is barely bubbling. Cover and simmer for 2 hours, then uncover and add the grated carrot. Continue to cook for a further 1 hour, stirring the pan occasionally to make sure the soup does not stick to the base as it thickens. The soup is ready when the lentils and split peas have turned into a purée. Taste and add more seasonings if required. Remove the sprig of parsley before serving.

Leftover soup can have a tablespoon of tomato purée added, together with half a cup of water to thin it down before reheating.

BORSCHT ON THE ROCKS

SERVES 6
COOKED BEET JUICE KEEPS FOR 4 DAYS IN THE FRIDGE, COMPLETE SOUP
FOR 2 DAYS | FREEZES FOR 3 MONTHS

A chilled glass of that heart-of-the-winter favourite, beetroot borscht, makes a superb non-alcoholic aperitif to a summer lunch. If you prefer, you can serve a larger quantity as a cold starter for the meal. Calories can be trimmed by substituting Greek yogurt or fromage frais for the more traditional soured cream.

2 bunches of young beetroots, or 600g/1lb 5oz old beetroots

1 onion

1 carrot

1L/1¾ pints hot water plus 2 vegetable stock cubes

10 grinds of black pepper

1 tbsp sugar or granular substitute

TO THICKEN

2 tbsp lemon juice

2 eggs

100ml/3½fl oz soured cream, Greek yogurt or creamy fromage frais

Have ready a large saucepan. Trim the beets, wash thoroughly and peel only if old. Peel the onion and the carrot. Cut all the vegetables into roughly 2.5cm/1 in chunks, then process in two batches until very finely chopped. Put in the pan with the water, pepper and sugar or sweetener. Bring to the boil, cover and simmer for 20 minutes until the vegetables are soft and the liquid is a rich, dark red.

Pour the contents through a coarse strainer into a bowl and discard the vegetables. Return the strained beet juice to the pan and leave on a low heat. Put the lemon juice and eggs into the food processor and process for 5 seconds until well mixed. With the motor running, pour two ladles of the hot beet juice through the feed tube and process for a further 3 seconds, then add to the beet juice in the pan and heat gently, whisking constantly with a batter whisk or balloon whisk until the soup is steaming and has thickened slightly. Do not let it boil or it will curdle. Taste and adjust the seasoning so that there is a gentle blend of sweet and sour.

Cool, then chill thoroughly. Just before serving, whisk in the cream, yogurt or fromage frais.

TARATOUR
HERBED YOGURT AND CUCUMBER SOUP

SERVES 6
KEEPS FOR 3 DAYS IN THE FRIDGE | DO NOT FREEZE

The herbs can be from the garden or the supermarket but use them fresh rather than dried for this delicate Israeli summer soup. Smetana is a Jewish soured cream – you can use soured cream or crème fraîche if you cannot obtain it.

275ml/10fl oz semi-skimmed milk

425ml/15fl oz natural yogurt

150ml/5fl oz Greek yogurt or smetana

1 cucumber

1 small bunch of radishes

2 tbsp snipped chives

2 heaped tbsp dill leaves, or
1 heaped tbsp chopped parsley

2 sprigs of tarragon

1 small bunch of very fresh, young mint leaves

1/2 tsp salt

10 grinds of black pepper

In a large jug or lipped bowl, gently stir together the milk and yogurts (or smetana, if using). Peel the cucumber and cut into matchsticks. Trim the radishes and slice very thinly. Snip the chives and dill or parsley and chop the tarragon and mint.

Stir all these into the yogurt mixture, together with the salt and pepper, cover and refrigerate until well chilled. Stir before serving.

SOUPE AU CRESSON
WATERCRESS SOUP

SERVES 6
KEEPS FOR 2 DAYS IN THE FRIDGE | PURÉE FREEZES FOR 2 MONTHS

The slightly acidic, tangy taste of watercress is especially delicious in a cold soup but equally good when hot. You can use less, but the three bunches suggested do produce a soup to remember.

250g/9oz watercress (about 3 small bunches)

40g/1½oz/3 tbsp butter

1 onion, finely chopped

white part of 1 fat leek, finely sliced

450g/1 lb potatoes, thinly sliced

1.2l/2 pints vegetable stock

1 bay leaf

1½–2 tsp salt

15 grinds of black pepper

275ml/10fl oz milk

150ml/5fl oz soured cream, or strained Greek natural yogurt

TO SERVE

leaves from reserved watercress, finely chopped

2½ tbsp pine nuts or flaked almonds, toasted in a dry pan

Wash and spin dry all the watercress, then cut off the leaves from one bunch, rewrap and refrigerate.

Melt the butter in a soup pan, add the onion and leek and sauté, covered, for 2 minutes until soft and golden. Add the potatoes, stock, bay leaf and seasonings, bring to the boil, cover and simmer for 20 minutes until the potatoes are tender. Add the remaining watercress, stalks as well as leaves, bring to the boil and simmer, uncovered, for 2 minutes.

Purée in a blender or food processor or in the pan with a stick blender until absolutely smooth. Return the purée to the rinsed pan and bring slowly to simmering point, then stir in the milk, remove from the heat and leave, covered until cool enough to refrigerate. Pour into a large bowl or jug, cover with cling film and chill for at least 12 hours.

To serve, stir in the reserved chopped watercress leaves and the cream or yogurt, taste and add extra salt if necessary. Garnish each serving with a scattering of pine nuts or flaked almonds.

HUNGARIAN CHERRY SOUP

SERVES 4
KEEPS FOR 3 DAYS IN THE FRIDGE | FREEZES WITHOUT
THE CREAM FOR 3 MONTHS

Fruit soup can be made with a combination of fruits, including peaches, plums, cherries or nectarines. It is then slightly thickened and enriched with smetana, or East European soured cream. The finest variety of fruit soup, however, is *Yayin Duvdivanim*. Made with Morello cherries, it is known in its birth place, Budapest, as *Hideg Meggyleves*. Serve the soup as you would borscht on the rocks (see page 42) as a starter in a glass. The flavour is best if the soup is prepared one day ahead.

1 lb 1oz (480g) jar pitted Morello cherries in syrup (reserve a few for garnish)

water, as needed

150ml/4³⁄₄fl oz Port or red Kiddush wine

125g/4¹⁄₂oz sugar

grated zest of ¹⁄₂ lemon

¹⁄₂ tsp salt

1 cinnamon stick

1 tbsp cornflour mixed to a cream with 1 tsp lemon juice and 1 tbsp water

200ml/6³⁄₄fl oz soured cream or smetana

Drain the cherries, reserving the syrup. Measure the syrup in a measuring jug and add enough water to make 750ml/1 ¹⁄₄ pint liquid.

Put the syrup mixture, wine, sugar, lemon zest, salt and cinnamon stick into a soup pan, bring to the boil and bubble uncovered for 7 minutes until the liquid is well flavoured. Add the cherries and the cornflour cream, bring back to the boil and simmer for 3 minutes until clear.

Cool until it stops steaming, then refrigerate until absolutely cold. Put the soured cream in a bowl and add a ladle or two of the cold cherry mixture, whisking until smooth. Pour this creamy liquid back into the cherry mixture and chill until just before serving. Serve cold but not icy, garnished with a few of the reserved cherries.

CHILLED SUMMER FRUIT SOUP

SERVES 6–8

KEEPS FOR 3 DAYS IN THE FRIDGE | FREEZES FOR 3 MONTHS

German Jews who summered, before the Second World War, in cottages on the shores of the Baltic, made marvellous cold soups from the fruits of high summer. The choice of ingredients depends on the season, but this combination of the sweet and the tart is particularly refreshing.

225g/8oz pitted fresh plums

225g/8oz pitted Morello or other tart cherries

225g/8oz sliced peaches

1.5l/2½ pints water

1 pinch of salt

small cinnamon stick or 1 tsp ground cinnamon

75g/3oz sugar

2 tbsp cornflour

1 tbsp water, or sweet red (Port-type) wine

150ml/5fl oz soured cream

Put the fruit, water, seasoning and sugar in a soup pan. Simmer, covered, for 15–20 minutes, or until the fruit is tender, then remove the cinnamon stick, if used, and force the mixture through a fine sieve, or purée in a blender (or in the pan with a stick blender) until smooth.

Mix the cornflour with a little water (or better still, sweet red wine), stir into the soup and simmer for 10 minutes until thickened and clear. Chill well.

Serve in soup cups, topped with soured cream, as a refreshing start to a summer meal.

POULTRY

OVEN-FRIED CHICKEN

SERVES 6
COOKED OR RAW CHICKEN FREEZES FOR 3 MONTHS

These crunchy portions of chicken are coated with a mixture of crumbs and herbs and are equally delicious hot or cold. They are cooked with only 5 tablespoons of oil, yet are as crisp as if they had been deep-fried. They make excellent 'freezer-fillers' because they can be frozen either cooked or ready-coated and raw.

5½ tbsp lemon juice

6 bone-in chicken portions, or boneless breasts, skinned

FOR THE COATING

6½ tbsp coating crumbs or medium matzah meal

1 egg, beaten

5½ tbsp sunflower oil

1 tsp salt

20 grinds of black pepper

3 tsp dried mixed herbs or Herbes de Provence (optional)

1 tsp paprika

¼ tsp garlic salt (optional)

finely grated zest of 1 lemon

Marinate the chicken 1 hour before cooking. Put the lemon juice into a flat dish, turn the chicken pieces in it, then leave. Turn once or twice.

Preheat the oven to 200°C/400°F/Gas 6. If you are using matzah meal or if the coating crumbs are pale in colour, spread them out on a baking sheet and put in the oven as it heats up until they are golden brown (this gives a better colour to the cooked chicken).

Whisk the egg and oil together with the salt and pepper until well blended and then put in a shallow dish large enough to hold a portion of chicken. Mix the coating crumbs, herbs, seasonings and lemon zest in a dish of a similar size. Have ready a lightly greased oven tray large enough to hold the portions, well spaced, side by side. Lay each chicken joint in the egg mixture, using a pastry brush to coat it evenly, then roll it in the crumb mixture, again to coat evenly. Pat off any excess with the hands.

Arrange on the baking sheet and cook for 40 minutes (30 minutes for boneless breasts) until a rich brown. There is no need to turn the chicken, as it will brown evenly on all sides. The chicken can be kept hot and crisp for up to 30 minutes in a warm oven at 100°C/200°F/Gas ½.

VARIATION
SESAME CHICKEN
Mix 75g/3oz sesame seeds with the coating crumbs or meal.

BIBLICAL CHICKEN

SERVES 6

KEEPS FOR 2 DAYS IN THE FRIDGE | FREEZES FOR 2 MONTHS

I have discovered that for boneless chicken breasts, the briefer the cooking period, the better. So to produce a tender yet juicy breast, I fry it lightly on both sides and then, after deglazing the pan, simply leave to soak in the sauce for 1 or 2 hours. It then needs only bringing slowly back to simmering point in the sauce before serving.

50g/2oz flaked almonds

6 part-boned chicken breasts, trimmed of ribcage and skinned

1½ tbsp flour

1 tsp salt

10 grinds of black pepper

50g/2oz/4 tbsp margarine and 1 tbsp sunflower or olive oil

FOR THE SAUCE

225ml/8fl oz dry white wine plus 125ml/4fl oz home-made chicken stock (see page 176), or 350ml/12fl oz chicken stock made with a stock cube

125ml/4fl oz orange juice

2 tsp grated lemon zest

1 tbsp clear honey

3 tbsp raisins, preferably muscatel (Muscat)

7.5cm/3in cinnamon stick

2 tsp cornflour mixed to a cream with 1 tbsp cold water or chicken stock

2 small oranges, peeled and cut into pith-free segments

Basmati rice or new potatoes, to serve

Take each breast in turn and flatten it gently between the hands. Season the flour with salt and pepper, then coat with the seasoned flour. In a large sauté pan, heat the fats until the foam subsides, then immediately add the almonds and cook gently until golden brown. Drain on a paper towel.

Add the chicken breasts to the hot fats – probably in 2 batches if the pan is small – and cook on each side for about 3 minutes, or until golden. Remove from the pan and pour away any excess fat without discarding the savoury brown bits at the bottom. Add the wine to the pan, stirring well, and bubble for 3 minutes to intensify the flavour, then add the stock, orange juice, lemon zest, honey, raisins and cinnamon stick. Bring the sauce to the boil, add the chicken breasts in a single layer, spoon the liquid over them, then cover the pan and take it off the heat.

Just before serving, bring the sauce slowly back to the simmer, add the cornflour cream and bubble for 3 minutes. Pierce a breast to check that there's no sign of pinkness; if there is, bubble for 3 more minutes. Lift the breasts out and arrange on a warm plate. Add salt and pepper if necessary, then spoon the sauce over the breasts and decorate the dish with the orange sections and the toasted almonds. Serve accompanied by Basmati rice or new potatoes.

POLLO EN PEPITORIA

SERVES 6
KEEPS FOR 2 DAYS IN THE FRIDGE | DO NOT FREEZE

This is a Spanish chicken dish that uses ground almonds to thicken the white wine sauce. The use of ground almonds as a thickener was common in medieval times, before the invention of a roux thickener. The chicken can be fried and the sauce prepared 1½ hours before serving.

50g/2oz flour

1 tsp salt

15 grinds of black pepper

6–8 chicken breasts, skinned, wing attached

4 tbsp olive oil

1 large onion, finely chopped

1 bay leaf

250ml/8½fl oz dry white wine plus 225ml/8fl oz home-made chicken stock (see page 176), or 500ml/ 17fl oz chicken stock made with a stock cube

50g/2oz ground almonds

2 hard-boiled egg yolks

1 fat garlic clove, halved

¼ tsp turmeric or ground saffron

TO SERVE

25g/1oz flaked almonds, toasted in a dry pan

1 hard-boiled egg, grated and mixed with 1 tbsp chopped parsley

Put the flour, salt and pepper into a plastic bag and shake the breasts in it, one at a time until evenly coated. Fry them in the hot oil a few at a time in a large sauté pan until a rich golden brown. Drain on paper towels and transfer to a baking tin large enough to hold them in a single layer.

To make the sauce, sauté the onion in the same oil, covering the pan until a rich gold and beginning to 'melt'. Add the bay leaf and wine and bubble, uncovered, for 3 minutes to concentrate the flavour. Then add the stock, cover and leave to simmer gently for 15 minutes.

Put the ground almonds, hard-boiled egg yolks, garlic and turmeric or saffron in the bowl of a food processor. Discard the bay leaf and process until pasty, then gradually add the simmering liquid and process until a smooth, creamy sauce is formed. Return to the saucepan, stir well and leave covered until just before serving.

To complete the cooking, preheat the oven to 190°C /375°F/Gas 5 and bake the chicken, uncovered, for 20 minutes until the juices run clear when the chicken is pierced with a sharp knife. Reheat the sauce gently until simmering. Arrange the chicken breasts on a heated platter and coat with the hot sauce. Scatter with the toasted almonds and the egg and parsley mixture.

CHICKEN IZMIR

SERVES 6
KEEPS FOR 2 DAYS IN THE FRIDGE | FREEZES FOR 3 MONTHS

This Turkish chicken dish with aubergine and warm spices is perfect for a spring dinner party. The sautéed aubergines give the sauce a distinctive rich, smooth flavour.

450g /1 lb aubergines, cut into 1 cm/½in cubes

1 tbsp salt

125ml/4fl oz sunflower oil

6 chicken joints, skinned

1 heaped tbsp flour

½ tsp salt

10 grinds of black pepper

1 tbsp olive oil

1 large onion, chopped

1 garlic clove, chopped

600 ml/1 pint vegetable stock

3 tbsp tomato purée

1 tsp salt

2 tsp brown sugar

10 grinds of black pepper

½ tsp ground cinnamon

½ tsp ground cumin

½ tsp ground coriander

Preheat the oven to 160°C /325°F/Gas 3.

Place the aubergine cubes in a bowl, cover with cold water and add the salt. Leave for half an hour and then squeeze out as much moisture as possible, or use a salad spinner. Put the sunflower oil in a large frying pan and heat for 3 minutes. Add the aubergine, cover and sauté on all sides until golden brown. Lift out and drain on kitchen paper.

Dry the chicken joints well and coat with the seasoned flour. In an oven-to-table casserole or sauté pan, fry the portions in the hot olive oil until they are a rich brown on all sides, then lift out and drain on paper towels to remove any surface fat.

In the same oil, gently sauté the chopped onion and garlic until they turn a rich brown. Keep the pan lid on for 5 minutes to soften them in the steam, then remove it to finish the browning.

Add the stock, tomato purée and seasonings. Stir well to release any tasty crispy bits adhering to the base of the casserole, then lay the chicken on top and surround with the fried aubergines. Bring to simmering point. Immediately cover and transfer to the oven. Bake for 50 minutes until the chicken is cooked through and the sauce is rich and thick.

SIRKE PAPRIKASH

SERVES 4
KEEPS FOR 3 DAYS IN THE FRIDGE | FREEZES FOR 2 MONTHS

This chicken paprika dish is the true Hungarian recipe. The quality of the paprika is the deciding factor in this simple but wonderfully flavoursome recipe, so buy the best quality you can find, ideally from a specialist spice shop. *Kulonleges* paprika, from Hungary, is the finest in quality and also the most finely ground.

1.5kg/3½lb chicken, backbone removed and cut into 4 portions on the bone, lightly salted

2 tbsp sunflower oil

1 onion, finely chopped

2 tbsp Hungarian paprika, preferably *Kulonleges*

150ml/5fl oz chicken stock

2 green or red peppers, deseeded and cut into fine 5mm/¼in strips

400g/14 oz canned chopped tomatoes

1 tsp cornflour mixed to a cream with 3 tbsp cold water

1 tsp salt

10 grinds of black pepper

Dry the chicken pieces with paper towels, then sauté in the hot oil until golden. Remove. In the remaining oil, gently cook the onion, covered, for 10–15 minutes until softened and golden.

Stir in the paprika and chicken stock and cook for a further 2 minutes. Add the chicken with any juices, the pepper strips and the tomatoes. Cover and cook very gently for 25–30 minutes until the chicken is cooked through – there will be no sign of pinkness when a piece is pierced with a sharp knife.

Lift the chicken pieces on to a warm platter. Add the cornflour mixture to the sauté pan. Simmer for 3 minutes, stirring, or until thickened to a coating consistency. Add the salt and pepper, taste and adjust the seasoning if necessary. Spoon the sauce over the chicken and serve.

KHORESH PORTAGAL
SWEET AND SOUR PERSIAN CHICKEN

SERVES 6
KEEPS FOR 2 DAYS IN THE FRIDGE | DO NOT FREEZE

Gently does it when cooking this exquisite chicken dish in a fruited sauce. The dish is adapted from medieval Persian cuisine, in which cubes of chicken breast meat are simmered in a lightly spiced orange sauce on the lowest possible heat until they are meltingly tender. Serve the khoresh with the wonderful Peersian chello rice (see page 170). It is equally delicious served at room temperature.

4 tbsp olive oil or sunflower oil

680g–1kg/1½–2¼lb well-dried chicken-breast meat, cut into 2.5cm/1in cubes

1½ tsp paprika

1½ tsp ground cinnamon

¼ tsp freshly grated nutmeg

½ tsp salt

8 grinds of black pepper

275ml/10fl oz chicken stock (see page 176)

1 large onion, finely sliced

25g/1oz/2 tbsp margarine

1 tsp oil

3 very large or 5 medium oranges, peeled and cut into pith-free segments

75g/3oz granulated sugar

5 tbsp white wine vinegar or cider vinegar

1½ tsp cornflour mixed to a cream with 1 tbsp water, if needed

Heat the oil and fry the chicken over a medium heat in a lidded sauté pan to seal it – it will turn white on all sides. Sprinkle on the spices and seasonings, mix well, cook a further 2 minutes and then add enough stock barely to cover the chicken. Cover and cook on the lowest possible heat – with the stock just bubbling – until tender and white all the way through, about 10 minutes.

Meanwhile, slowly sauté the onion in the margarine and oil until a rich, deep gold – don't over-brown, as it will impair the flavour. Put the oranges in another small saucepan, sprinkle with the sugar and vinegar and cook gently, uncovered, for 15 minutes or until the fruit is sitting in a thick syrup. Arrange the onion and its juices on top of the chicken, followed by the oranges and their syrup. Reheat very gently, covered, for 10 minutes. If the sauce seems thin, stir in the cornflour mixture and simmer, stirring, for a further 3 minutes until clear. The dish may be reheated.

SPICED CHICKEN PILAFF

SERVES 6

LEFTOVERS KEEP FOR 2 DAYS IN THE FRIDGE | FREEZE FOR 3 MONTHS

Really fresh and fragrant spices and a well-flavoured stock are the essential ingredients that can transform a mundane Monday dish such as pilaff into a party sparkler. In this version, a blend of wild and long-grain rice, available in ready-mixed packs, adds extra crunch. The elements of this richly satisfying dish can be cooked ahead and assembled just before serving.

1.5kg/3½lb chicken, quartered

575ml/1 pint water

1 onion

1 tsp salt

10 grinds of black pepper

large sprig parsley

250g/9oz mixed long-grain and wild rice

1 bay leaf

50g/2oz flaked almonds, toasted in a dry pan

2½ tbsp virgin olive oil

½ tsp sea salt

fresh coriander leaves or flat leaf parsley, chopped

FOR THE SAUCE

225ml/8fl oz home-made chicken stock (see page 176)

1 tsp ground cumin

2 tsp freshly ground coriander seeds

1 tsp freshly grated ginger

1 garlic clove, crushed with a little sea salt

16 grinds of black pepper

To cook the bird, put it in a pan with the water, onion, salt, pepper and parsley. Cover with foil and then a lid to keep in the steam and simmer very gently for 1 hour until absolutely tender.

Lift out the chicken, remove the skin and bones and cut the meat into bite-sized strips. Boil the stock, if necessary, down to 575ml/1 pint, then pour through a sieve and reserve.

To cook the rice, put it in a heavy-based saucepan with the bay leaf and reserved stock, cover and bring to the boil over a moderate heat. Stir well, reduce the heat and simmer for 20 minutes, or until the liquid has been absorbed and the rice is cooked but still has bite to it. Discard the bay leaf. Set aside.

To make the sauce put the home-made stock in a small saucepan over a moderate heat and stir in the cumin, coriander, ginger, garlic and seasoning. Simmer for 5 minutes, remove from the heat and set aside.

Just before serving, heat the olive oil in a large frying pan and tip in the cooked rice, toasted nuts and sea salt with enough of the reheated sauce to moisten. Turn the mixture around in the oil until heated through. Meanwhile, gently reheat the chicken either on the stove in a steamer lined with oiled foil, or covered, in the microwave for 2–3 minutes.

Arrange the chicken and rice on a large warmed serving dish, moisten with the sauce and scatter over the coriander or parsley. Serve, handing round any extra sauce separately.

MOROCCAN CHICKEN PILAFF WITH FRUIT AND NUTS

SERVES 6

KEEPS FOR 3 DAYS IN THE FRIDGE | FREEZES FOR 3 MONTHS

This pilaff can be cooked well ahead, then reheated in a moderate oven or the microwave, but the chicken does need to be stir-fried just before serving – it toughens when reheated.

125g/4½oz wild and brown rice mix

225g/8oz white Basmati rice

2 tbsp salt

2 tbsp sunflower or vegetable oil

1 bunch of spring onion bulbs, finely chopped

100g/4oz ready-to-eat dried apricots, chopped with kitchen scissors

50g/2oz shelled pistachios

50g/2oz pine nuts

2 tbsp ground cinnamon

1 tsp ground cumin

1 tsp salt

15 grinds of black pepper

500g/1lb 2oz chicken-breast meat, cut into 7.5 x 1cm/3 x ½in strips

salt and ground black pepper

3 tbsp lemon juice

1½ tbsp sunflower or vegetable oil

2 tsp ground cinnamon

To cook the rice, soak both sorts in cold water to cover for 30 minutes. Strain and rinse thoroughly under the tap until the water runs clear. Bring a large heavy saucepan of water to the boil with the salt. Add the rice and cook uncovered, bubbling steadily for 7 minutes, or until a grain feels almost tender when bitten. Turn into a strainer and rinse thoroughly under the hot tap, then drain well. Coat the bottom of the pan with 1 tablespoon of the oil, then add the rice. Wrap a tea towel under the lid of the pan, then place it firmly into position so that you have a perfect seal. Steam over the lowest possible heat for 20 minutes.

Meanwhile, put the remaining oil into a medium sauté pan and cook the onions briskly until golden, then add the apricots, pistachios and pine nuts, sprinkling them with 1½ tablespoons cinnamon and the cumin as they cook. Using a slotted spoon, remove this mixture from the pan and stir it into the cooked rice, together with the salt and pepper. Transfer to a microwave-safe dish. Season the chicken and sprinkle with the lemon juice. Set aside.

Just before serving, reheat the rice in the microwave, covered, on 100 per cent power for 2–3 minutes, then stir gently with a fork.

Meanwhile, stir-fry the chicken strips in the very hot sunflower or vegetable oil for 3 minutes, sprinkling them with the remaining cinnamon, then stir into the reheated rice. Serve on a shallow platter.

ROAST CHICKEN
WITH PINE NUTS

SERVES 6

KEEPS FOR 3 DAYS IN THE FRIDGE | FREEZES FOR 3 MONTHS

Strewing the breast of the bird with fresh herbs and adding a crunch of pine nuts to the gravy quite transforms plain roast chicken into something extra special.

2–2.25kg/5–5½lb roasting chicken

3 tbsp fresh lemon juice

1 eating apple

olive oil

sea salt

10 grinds of black pepper

12 shallots

3 tbsp chopped mixed herbs

4 tbsp pine nuts

125ml/4fl oz each dry white wine and chicken stock, or 225ml/8fl oz stock alone

2 tsp cornflour mixed to a cream with 3 tbsp cold water

1 small bunch of parsley

1 pinch of sugar (optional)

Preheat the oven to 190°C/375°F/Gas 5. Pat the cavity of the bird dry, squeeze the lemon juice into it, insert the unpeeled, quartered apple and carefully transfer the bird to a rack standing in a roasting tin, placing it breast-side down. Brush lightly with olive oil and sprinkle with ground sea salt and pepper.

Roast for 1 hour 20 minutes, basting every 20 minutes. Turn the bird over, breast-side up, and slip the shallots underneath the rack. Brush the breast lightly with olive oil, season again and strew with the chopped herbs. Roast for a further 40 minutes, basting once until the chicken is a rich golden brown, and the juices run clear when the leg is pierced with a skewer.

Meanwhile, sauté the pine nuts gently in a little oil until golden brown. Lift the bird on to a carving dish and leave in a warm place. Remove the shallots with a slotted spoon and keep hot. Put the roasting tin on top of the stove and drain off the fat from the dish. Add the pine nuts, wine and stock with the cornflour cream. Bubble for 3 minutes, stirring, taste and re-season if necessary. Stir in the parsley. (Add a pinch of sugar if too acidic.)

Portion or carve the bird and serve with the pine nuts and sauce. The golden-brown shallots can be served with the other vegetables.

ROAST TURKEY WITH A FRUITED BULGUR STUFFING

SERVES 4–6

LEFTOVERS KEEP FOR 3 DAYS IN THE FRIDGE | FREEZE FOR 3 MONTHS

2–2.5kg/4½lb–5½lb turkey

FOR THE STUFFING

60g/2oz dried apricots

60g/2oz dried pears

2 tbsp olive oil

1 onion, chopped

1 large garlic clove, chopped

1 tbsp finely chopped fresh ginger

175g/6oz bulgur wheat

700ml/1½ pints good chicken stock

25g/1oz pine nuts, lightly toasted in a dry pan

½ tsp freshly grated nutmeg

finely grated zest of 2 lemons

1 tsp salt

10 grinds of black pepper

FOR THE GLAZE

2 tbsp clear honey

2 tbsp fresh lemon juice

First prepare the stuffing. Cover the dried fruit with boiling water and leave to plump up for 30 minutes.

Next, heat half the olive oil in a lidded sauté pan and cook the onion and garlic for 5 minutes until a rich gold. Stir in the ginger and cook for a further minute, then add the bulgur, coating it well with the oil. Add 1.2l/2 pints of the hot stock and the coarsely chopped dried fruit, cover and cook over very low heat for about 10 minutes, or until the liquid has been absorbed. Stir in the pine nuts, nutmeg, lemon zest, salt and pepper. Set to one side.

Preheat the oven to 230°C/450°F/Gas 8. Fill the cavity of the bird loosely with some of the stuffing, then tie the legs together to make it a compact shape. Oil a roasting tin and set a rack in it, then arrange the bird on top and brush all over with the remaining oil. Put the remaining stuffing in an oven-proof dish, cover tightly and set aside. Put the bird in the oven, then turn the temperature down to 190°C/375°F/Gas 5. Roast the bird, allowing 20 minutes for each 450g/1lb, based on its weight before stuffing.

While the bird is roasting, mix together the honey and lemon juice. Thirty minutes before the bird is done, brush all over with glaze, and put the dish with the bulgur in the oven to cook. After a further 15 minutes, brush again with the glaze, and brush again when the bird is cooked. Transfer a warm dish to rest.

Meanwhile, pour the remaining stock into the roasting tin and stir well over moderate heat, then pour the liquid through a sieve into a saucepan. Skim off as much fat as possible, then boil down until it is smooth and well seasoned. Serve hot with the sliced bird and the stuffing.

HAIMISCHE CASSEROLED FOWL

SERVES 4–6, DEPENDING ON THE SIZE OF THE BIRD
LEFTOVERS KEEP FOR 3 DAYS IN THE FRIDGE | FREEZE FOR 3 MONTHS

Fowls are specially bred for the Jewish market and are available from kosher butchers. They are about 12 months old, firm-fleshed and mature enough to make excellent soup, yet still young enough to be tender and flavoursome in stews. A fine plump fowl has, perhaps, more flavour than any other kind of bird. This is the ultimate comfort-food casserole.

1 tsp salt

10 grinds of black pepper

2 tsp flour

2 tsp paprika

1 fowl, 2–2.25kg/4½–5½lb, made kosher and scalded

1 tbsp oil

1 large onion, thinly sliced

1 garlic clove, crushed

1 bay leaf

1 carrot, thinly sliced

2 soft tomatoes, or
2½ tbsp tomato purée

125ml/4fl oz home-made chicken stock (see page 176) or traditional chicken soup (see page 34)

any or all of the following vegetables:

½ red or yellow pepper, deseeded and cut into strips

3 celery stalks, diced

125g/4oz mushrooms, sliced

Preheat the oven to 180°C /350°F/Gas 4. Mix the salt, pepper, flour and paprika, then rub into the bird's skin.

In a heavy casserole, heat the oil and fry the onion and garlic until soft and golden, then add the bay leaf and all the remaining vegetables and stir over a gentle heat until they have absorbed most of the fat. Put the bird in and turn it in the hot fat until it goes pale gold. Pour the stock or soup down the side of the casserole. Cover and transfer to the oven.

After 15 minutes, turn the oven down to 160°C/325°F/Gas 3 and cook for 3 hours, or until the bird is a rich golden brown and the leg can be moved easily in its socket. During cooking, the liquid should be bubbling very gently. If bubbling is too violent, turn the oven down to 150°C/300°F/Gas 2. Baste twice with the pan juices.

To serve, lift the bird on to a warm platter. Skim off as much fat as possible. Remove the bay leaf, then blend or process the vegetables and liquid until absolutely smooth – this produces a marvellous naturally thickened gravy. Bring to the boil, taste and re-season if necessary, then serve.

DUCK BREASTS WITH A HONEY AND GINGER GLAZE

SERVES 6

LEFTOVERS KEEP FOR 3 DAYS IN THE FRIDGE | FREEZE FOR 2 MONTHS

This recipe produces a duck in the Chinese style with a mahogany brown, crunchy skin. No sauce is necessary, but a fruity salad of chicory and orange makes a refreshing accompaniment.

6 large duck breasts, on the bone

young fresh ginger

freshly ground black pepper

juice of 1 small orange

2½ tbsp clear honey

2 tsp soy sauce

1 pinch of salt

a salad of orange segments, chicory and a sprinkling of sesame seeds, to serve (optional)

Remove any lumps of fat from the duck joints and prick all over, piercing only the skin, not the flesh. Peel, then finely chop enough of the ginger to make 2 rounded tablespoons.

Lay the duck joints side by side in a large dish, scatter with the ginger and sprinkle with the black pepper, rubbing in well. Pour over the orange juice, then turn the joints to make sure they are evenly moistened on all sides. Cover and set aside for several hours in a cool place, or overnight in the fridge.

To cook the duck breasts, preheat the oven to 200°C/400°F/Gas 6. Drain the marinade from the duck and scrape off the ginger, then mix them together and reserve.

Arrange the breasts on a rack in a roasting tin and roast for 15 minutes. Mix the honey – or creamy honey heated until runny – with the marinade and stir in the soy sauce and salt.

Pour off all the fat that has collected under the duck, then paint the portions all over with the glaze. Roast for another 10 minutes, basting once. At the end of this time the duck should be a mahogany brown and deliciously tender. If it seems to be browning too quickly, cover loosely with a tent of foil.

MEAT

CHOLENT

SERVES 6
KEEPS FOR 3 DAYS IN THE FRIDGE | LEFTOVERS FREEZE FOR 3 MONTHS

This dish goes by several names – *cholent*, *sholent* or *shalet* to name a few – and the ingredients, though basically meat, potatoes and fat, vary according to the whim and location of the cook. But, as one Jewish cookery writer puts it, this ancient Sabbath recipe is best defined as 'any dish that has the stamina to stand up to 24 hours in the oven'.

450g/1lb dried butter beans

1.75kg/4lb piece of boneless brisket

½ tsp salt

20 grinds of pepper

1 tsp paprika

1 tsp ground ginger

2 tbsp chicken fat or margarine

3 onions, sliced

1 garlic clove, crushed

1 bay leaf

6 peeled whole potatoes or 225g/8oz pearl barley

If the dish is to be served as an accompaniment rather than a main course, use only 225g/8oz butter beans, 225g/8oz beef and a knuckle bone, if available, for flavour.

Soak the butter beans in enough cold water to cover overnight, then drain well. Preheat the oven to 200°C/400°F/Gas 6.

Rub the brisket with the salt, pepper, paprika and ginger, then brown quickly in the chicken fat or margarine, together with the onions and garlic. Put in a deep earthenware casserole (a hot-pot or Dutch oven is ideal). Add the bay leaf, drained and soaked beans and the potatoes or barley.

Cover with boiling water, put a lid on the dish and place in the oven for 30 minutes, or until the contents start to bubble. Turn the heat right down to 110°C/225°F/Gas ½, and leave overnight. Serve for lunch the next day.

BRAISED BRISKET POT ROAST

SERVES 4–6, PLUS LEFTOVERS FOR SANDWICHES
COOKED MEAT KEEPS FOR 3 DAYS IN THE FRIDGE | FREEZES FOR 3 MONTHS

One of the tastiest of kosher cuts. Leftover brisket should be forced into a bowl, covered with a saucer and a 1kg (2¼lb) weight, and then refrigerated. Next day it will cut to perfection.

1.5kg/3lb corner of brisket

1 tbsp sunflower oil or olive oil

1 bay leaf

6 peppercorns

2 tsp salt

10 grinds of black pepper

6 pickling onions or shallots

185ml/6fl oz boiling water

2 large potatoes

2 carrots

Preheat the oven to at 150°C /300°F/Gas 2.

Brown the meat quickly in the hot oil. Sprinkle with the seasonings. Put in a casserole surrounded with the peeled onions or shallots and the boiling water. Cover and cook in the oven for 3 hours.

An hour before the meat is ready, surround it with thick slices of potato and carrot. Serve the brisket cut into thick slices, together with the potatoes and carrots, in the delicious meat juices.

TSIMMES

SERVES 6 AS A MAIN COURSE, 8 AS A SIDE DISH – BUT YOU CAN NEVER MAKE ENOUGH TSIMMES TO SATISFY EVERYONE

A tsimmes – a sweet carrot and brisket casserole – might be called a Jewish hotpot, for its flavour depends on long, slow cooking during which the sweet elements in it – be they carrots, dried fruits, sweet potatoes, squash, honey or golden syrup – slowly caramelize, giving rise to a glorious aroma.

900g/2lb slice of brisket, excess fat trimmed and cut into 4cm/1 ½in chunks

1.5kg/3½lb carrots, peeled and cut into 1.25cm/½in cubes

4 slightly rounded tbsp golden syrup

½ tsp white pepper

2 tsp salt

1 tbsp cornflour mixed to a cream with 2 tbsp water

680g/1½lb potatoes, peeled and cut into large cubes

FOR THE DUMPLING (OPTIONAL)

6 tbsp margarine

175g/6oz self-raising flour

½ tsp salt

5–6 tbsp water or extra to mix

Put the carrots and meat into a pan, barely cover with hot water, add 2 tablespoons of the syrup, the pepper and ½ teaspoon of the salt, bring to the boil, and simmer for 2 hours either on top of the stove or in a slow oven. Skim or, if possible, chill overnight, so that most of the fat can be removed.

Four hours before you want to serve the tsimmes, make the dumpling by rubbing the margarine into the flour and salt. Gradually add the water and mix to a dough. Put the dumpling in the middle of a large oval earthenware, enamel or enamelled-iron casserole. Lift the meat and carrots from their cooking liquid with a slotted spoon and arrange around the dumpling.

Preheat the oven to 150°C/300°F/Gas 2. Stir the cornflour cream into the stock from the carrots and meat. Bring to the boil, stirring, then pour over the carrots and meat. Arrange the potatoes on top, adding extra boiling water if necessary so that they are just submerged. Sprinkle with the remaining salt and syrup. Cover and bring to the boil on top of the stove (taking care that the bottom of the dumpling does not burn), then transfer to the oven and cook for 3½ hours.

Uncover and taste, adding a little more syrup if necessary. Allow to brown for a further half an hour, then serve.

STUFATO DI MANZO FIORENTINA

FLORENTINE BEEF STEW WITH RED WINE AND ROSEMARY

SERVES 4-6
KEEPS FOR 3 DAYS IN THE FRIDGE | FREEZES FOR 3 MONTHS

2 garlic cloves, finely chopped

I tsp fresh or dried rosemary, finely chopped or crumbled

3 tbsp olive oil

1.25kg/2½lb braising or stewing steak, cut in to 2.5cm/1in chunks

I tsp salt

10 grinds of black pepper

2 tsp brown sugar

250ml/9fl oz dry red wine

150ml/5fl oz beef stock

4 tbsp tomato purée

I tsp dried Italian seasoning herbs

I tbsp chopped parsley

I tbsp chopped fresh basil

TO SERVE

350g/12oz (uncooked weight) penne or fusilli

Gently sauté the garlic and rosemary in the oil to flavour it. Dry the meat well with kitchen paper. Sauté the well-dried meat in the flavoured oil until it is richly browned all over, sprinkling it with the salt, pepper and sugar. Don't crowd the pan – if necessary, fry the meat in 2 batches.

Pour in the wine and bubble fiercely for 3 minutes to concentrate the flavour, then add the stock, tomato purée and dried herbs. Cover and simmer for 2 hours on top of the stove, or 2½ hours in the oven at 150°C/ 300°F /Gas 2. The meat should be bathed in a thick sauce. Stir in the parsley and basil.

Serve with the pasta, cooked according to packet directions.

PAN-SEARED RIB STEAK

SERVES 4

Kosher steaks are best when seared on the stove, either in a heavy-based frying pan or preferably, in a ridged stove-top cast-iron grill pan. To ensure tenderness, ask the butcher to cut the steaks from a side of beef that has been hung for 7–10 days. To ensure perfectly cooked steak, use an instant-read meat thermometer. The temperature continues to rise as the meat rests, so remove it from the heat when it reaches 5 degrees below your target temperature (e.g. 55°C/130°F for medium-rare).

4 rib steaks (entrecôtes), 175–225g/6–8oz each and 2–2.5cm/¾–1 in thick

black pepper

sunflower or vegetable oil

FOR THE SAUCE

150ml/5fl oz dry white or red wine or white vermouth, or the same amount of gravy left over from a roast or a braise, or good-quality stock

2 tsp dark soy sauce

a few grinds of black pepper

1 tsp sea salt

1 tbsp chopped parsley

Take the steaks from the fridge 1 hour before cooking. Trim most of the fat from each steak, leaving only a very thin edging. Dry well with paper towels. Sprinkle with freshly ground black pepper.

Heat the pan over a high heat until a sprinkling of water sizzles and evaporates as soon as it hits the surface (it should be extremely hot). Brush very lightly with oil using a piece of paper towel, then put in the steaks. Sear the meat for 3–4 minutes, then turn and cook on the other side for a further 4–6 minutes, turning the steaks again if necessary. Check the temperature with a meat thermometer, or pierce one steak and if it's the right colour in the centre, immediately transfer to a warm plate and leave to rest while you make the sauce.

Turn down the heat and add the liquid to the pan. Swirl this round to loosen the delicious sediment sticking to the bottom; if using a ridged pan, you may find a small silicone brush helpful for this. Allow to simmer for a minute or so until slightly reduced to concentrate the flavour. Add the soy sauce and seasonings, then pour over the steak and serve at once.

ALBONDIGAS AL BUYOR
GREEK-JEWISH MEATBALLS IN A SWEET-AND-SOUR SAUCE

SERVES 4
KEEPS FOR 4 DAYS IN THE FRIDGE | FREEZES FOR 3 MONTHS

FOR THE MEATBALLS

2 large egg

1 slice white or brown bread, 2.5cm/1in thick and torn into pieces

½ small onion

½ tsp salt

7 grinds of black pepper

1½ tsp dark soy sauce

1 large sprig of parsley

500g/1½ lb raw minced beef

1 tbsp flour mixed with a pinch of salt and pepper

3 tbsp sunflower or vegetable oil

FOR THE SAUCE

1 onion, finely chopped

2 tsp salt

10 grinds of black pepper

3 tbsp brown sugar or 2 tbsp clear honey

2 tsp Dijon or English mustard

2 tsp soy sauce

1 tbsp lemon juice

150g/5oz tomato purée, diluted with 225ml/8fl oz water

For the basic meatballs, mix the eggs, bread torn into pieces, onion, seasonings and parsley in a food processor for 30 seconds, or until smooth. Mix the raw meat and the egg mixture with your hands or a large fork until smoothly blended. Leave for 30 minutes.

With wet hands, shape the mixture into patties or balls, and cook as required.

Put the seasoned flour on to a piece of paper, and dip each patty into it. Shake off any excess flour.

Heat the oil in a heavy frying pan for 4 minutes, put in the meatballs and fry steadily until they are a rich brown on both sides.

To make the sauce, remove the fried meatballs, and in the same fat, sauté the onion until golden. Add all the remaining ingredients and simmer for 5 minutes.

Place the meatballs in a casserole, pour over the sauce and cover. Either simmer on the top of the stove for 30 minutes or bake in a slow oven at 150°C/300°F/Gas 2 for 45 minutes.

GEFILTE PAPRIKA
STUFFED PEPPERS, HUNGARIAN STYLE

SERVES 4–6
KEEPS FOR 3 DAYS IN THE FRIDGE | FREEZES FOR 2 MONTHS

This recipe is a more sophisticated version than often found – note the wine in the sauce, reflecting the cuisine soignée ('cooking with care'), typical of this part of Europe.

FOR THE SAUCE

1 onion, chopped

1 tbsp oil

150g/5oz tomato purée

275ml/10fl oz hot water

3 tbsp demerara sugar

3 tbsp lemon juice

1/2 tsp mixed spice or ground cinnamon

150ml/5fl oz white wine (optional but nice) or water

FOR THE PEPPERS AND STUFFING

4–6 squat sweet red peppers

1 egg, beaten

1 onion, grated

1 tsp salt

1/2 tsp mustard

1 tsp paprika

450g/1lb lean minced beef

2 tsp matzah meal or porridge oats

If the peppers are to be stewed on top of the stove, use the same pan to make the sauce. Fry the onion in the oil until soft and golden. Add all the remaining ingredients. Simmer, uncovered, for 20 minutes.

Slice off and retain the tops of the peppers and remove the seeds and ribs. Put into a saucepan and pour boiling water over the top, then leave for 5 minutes. Mix the egg, onion salt, mustard and paprika. Then mix in the meat and meal.

Drain the peppers on kitchen paper, then stuff with the meat mixture and cover each pepper with its top. Put into the pan in which the sauce is simmering. Cover with foil, and then with the lid of the pan. Simmer gently for 1 hour, basting twice. When done, the sauce will be thick and the peppers tender.

Alternatively, cook in the oven at 170°C/325°F/Gas 3 for 1 1/2 hours.

To cook in the microwave, mix the sauce ingredients in a jug and cook uncovered on 100 per cent (1000W) power for 3 minutes or until bubbling. Arrange the stuffed peppers in a 3l/5 pint deep, lidded casserole large enough to hold the peppers side by side. Pour the sauce round them and cook on 100 per cent (1000W) power for 6 minutes, or until bubbling, then reduce to 40 per cent power and cook for a further 15 minutes or until the peppers feel tender when pierced with a sharp knife. Stand for 5 minutes before serving.

SEPHARDI-STYLE PIZZA

SERVES 6 | MAKES 2 X 25CM/10IN PIZZAS
OVEN-READY PIZZA FREEZES FOR 3 MONTHS

Middle Eastern Jews have been making this very special version of pizza for centuries. It is made, of course, without cheese and is topped instead with cumin-scented minced beef. Defrost frozen pizzas at room temperature for 2 hours, then bake as though freshly prepared.

FOR THE PIZZA DOUGH

7g/¼oz/2 tsp easy-blend yeast or 14g/½oz/¼ cake fresh yeast

300g/11 oz plain flour

1½ tsp salt

1½ tsp sugar

3 tbsp olive oil

1 egg

150ml/5fl oz hand-hot water

FOR THE TOPPING

1 onion, finely chopped

2 tbsp olive oil

450g/1lb lean minced beef

1 tbsp tomato purée

1 tsp brown sugar

1 tsp salt

10 grinds of black pepper

1 tsp ground allspice

1 tsp ground cumin

1 good pinch of Cayenne pepper or chilli flakes

3 tbsp chopped parsley

1 tbsp lemon juice

125g/4½oz frying wurst (kosher beef salami)

If using easy-blend yeast, mix with the flour, salt and sugar; if using fresh yeast, dissolve it in the water. Mix all the ingredients together to form a soft but non-sticky ball of dough (add some extra flour if necessary); knead by hand or machine until smooth.

Put the dough in an oiled mixing bowl, turn it over so that it is coated with the oil, then cover with cling film and leave in the kitchen until double in bulk – about 1 hour.

To make the filling, cook the finely chopped onions in the oil, covered, until softened and golden, then mix in a bowl with all the remaining ingredients except the wurst, using the hands to make sure the mixture is evenly blended together.

Preheat the oven to 230°C/450°F/Gas 8. Grease two baking sheets or 25cm/10in pizza pans. Divide the risen dough in half, knead each portion for 1–2 minutes to distribute the gas bubbles evenly, then roll or press out into 2 x 25cm/10in rounds and place on the baking sheets or in the pizza pans.

Spread each round with an even layer of the filling, making sure the dough is covered right to the edges, then decorate with finely sliced wurst. Bake for 15 minutes until the meat is a rich brown and the wurst has curled. Serve at once.

PASTELES

The filling of these Sephardi meat pies is seasoned with allspice and contains fried pine nuts, which give them a satisfying texture.

FOR THE MEAT FILLING

25g/1oz/2 tbsp pine nuts

1 tbsp sunflower oil

1 onion, finely chopped

450g/1lb minced beef or lamb

100ml/3½fl oz plus 1 tbsp cold water

½ tsp ground cinnamon

½ tsp ground allspice

1 tsp salt

10 grinds of black pepper

FOR THE PASTRY

350g/12oz plain flour, plus extra for dusting

1 tsp salt

175g/6oz baking margarine, cut into chunks

2 tbsp sunflower oil

about 5 tbsp warm water

FOR THE TOPPING

1 egg, beaten

sesame seeds

Fry the pine nuts gently in the oil until brown, then drain. Put the chopped onion into the pan and brown gently, add the meat and continue to cook until it is brown all over. Barely cover with water, add the seasonings and simmer, uncovered, until the moisture has almost evaporated and the meat looks juicy. Stir in the pine nuts.

To make the pastry and shape the pasteles, put the flour, salt and margarine in a large bowl and sprinkle with the oil. Rub in the fat. Sprinkle with enough of the water to make a firm but non-sticky dough.

Preheat the oven to 400°F/200°C/Gas 6. Roll out the pastry 2.5mm/⅛in thick on a lightly floured board and, using metal pastry cutters, cut the dough into 16 x 8–9cm/3½–4in rounds and 16 x 5cm/2in rounds. Place the larger circles of pastry in patty tins, add a spoonful of cooled meat mixture, moisten the edges and top with the smaller round, sealing the edges.

Alternatively, to shape the cases in the traditional Sephardi way, use your fingers to pleat the edges of the larger circles to form cups 2cm/¾in deep. Fill with the cooled meat, then moisten the edges, place a small circle on top and press the two together with your thumbs to seal in the meat. Arrange on ungreased baking sheets about 2.5cm/1in apart.

Whichever way you shape them, brush the filled pies with beaten egg and scatter with sesame seeds. Bake for 20–25 minutes, or until a rich brown.

LE GIGOT QUI PLEURE

SERVES 6
LEFTOVERS KEEP FOR 3 DAYS IN THE FRIDGE | FREEZE FOR 3 MONTHS

This recipe for Kosher-style rolled shoulder of lamb, the aroma is intensified by spiking the meat with rosemary several hours before cooking. The exotic names comes from the meat juices dripping into the vegetables.

1.5kg/3lb boned and rolled shoulder of lamb

2 sprigs fresh rosemary

2 garlic cloves, slivered

TO COAT THE LAMB

20 grinds of black pepper

olive oil

1 tsp mustard powder

1 tbsp flour

2 tbsp demerara sugar

TO COOK BENEATH THE LAMB

750g/1lb 10oz small new potatoes, scrubbed

1 tsp salt

350g/12oz shallots

575ml/1 pint meat stock (see page 176)

FOR THE SAUCE

juices from the roasting tin, made up to 275ml/10fl oz with hot water

90ml/3½fl oz plus 1 tbsp red wine mixed with 1 tbsp cornflour

Several hours in advance, pierce the lamb at 5cm/2in intervals, and in each incision insert a tiny sprig of rosemary and a sliver of garlic.

Preheat the oven to 180°C/350°F/Gas 4. Sprinkle the lamb with pepper, brush with olive oil and sprinkle with the mixed mustard and flour, then arrange on a rack that fits 5cm/2in above a roasting tin.

Put the potatoes into a saucepan of cold water, add the salt and bring to the boil. Lift out with a slotted spoon and arrange in the roasting tin. In the same water, bring the shallots to the boil, then turn into a sieve and drench with cold water. The skins can now be easily removed. Arrange with the potatoes in the roasting tin. Make the stock with boiling water, then pour over and around the potatoes and shallots. Lay the meat on its rack on top of the vegetables, put in the oven and cook for 2¼ hours.

After 1 hour, take out the roasting tin and lift off the meat on its rack so that you can stir the vegetables. Replace the meat, sprinkle with the sugar and return to the oven. Check after half an hour, and if the stock seems to be drying up, add a little more hot water.

Lift the meat out on to a dish and leave to stand, loosely covered with foil, or in the oven turned to its lowest setting. Lift out the vegetables with a slotted spoon and put into a dish. Cover and keep warm.

FOR THE SAUCE
Put the roasting tin on the stove and add the boiling water, then stir well to release all the delicious sediment. Mix the cornflour to a smooth cream with the wine and add to the pan. Bubble for 3 minutes, stirring well, and taste and re-season if needed. (At this stage you may wish to transfer the sauce to a small saucepan to keep hot.) Allow the meat to stand for 20 minutes before slicing and serving.

ROAST STUFFED LAMB WITH APRICOT OR MINT STUFFING

SERVES 6–8

LEFTOVERS KEEP FOR 3 DAYS IN THE FRIDGE | RAW STUFFING FREEZES FOR 1 MONTH

Using a 1.5kg/3½lb shoulder of lamb, this recipe produces a particularly succulent joint that is equally delicious cold.

1.5kg/3½lb shoulder of lamb

APRICOT STUFFING

4 tbsp margarine

1 small onion, finely chopped

125g/4oz dried apricots, soaked overnight in cold water then drained, or ready-eat apricots, roughly chopped

grated zest of ½ lemon

½ tsp salt

1 pinch of white pepper

125g/4oz fresh breadcrumbs

1 egg, beaten

MINT STUFFING

4 tbsp margarine

1 small onion, chopped

175g/6oz fresh breadcrumbs

2 tsp each finely chopped mint and parsley

1 tsp salt

¼ tsp black pepper

1 egg, beaten

Ask the butcher to bone the meat, if possible leaving a pocket for the stuffing. If this is not possible, the boned meat can be spread with the stuffing, then rolled before roasting.

To make either stuffing, melt the fat in a small frying pan and cook the onion gently until softened and golden. Put all the other ingredients into a bowl, except the egg, then mix in the onion and fat until well blended. Moisten with the beaten egg. The mixture should just cling together.

To stuff a pocketed shoulder, just pack the stuffing lightly into the pocket and sew it up into a firm, compact shape using a large needle and twine. To stuff and roll a shoulder, lay the meat, skin-side down, on a board and cut out any lumps of fat. Spread the stuffing evenly over the meat, pushing it into any little folds. Roll up neatly and sew into a compact shape, or skewer closed if this is possible.

To roast the meat, preheat the oven to 180°C/350°F/Gas 4. Put a rack in a roasting tin and lay the meat on top. Sprinkle with the salt and pepper for the coating, dust lightly with flour, then pour over the oil. Roast the meat for 2 hours, then sprinkle with the sugar and increase the heat to 200°C/400°F/Gas 6. Cook for a further 20–30 minutes until a rich brown. Leave to rest in a warm place (or in the oven turned down to 110°C/225°F/Gas ¼ for 15 minutes before carving).

Continued on page 83

FOR THE COATING

1 tsp salt

10 grinds of black pepper

dusting of flour

2 tbsp oil

1 tbsp demerara sugar

FOR THE GRAVY

275ml/10 fl oz water

2 tsp cornflour

1 beef stock cube

For the gravy, pour off all but 2 teaspoons of fat from the roasting tin. Mix the cold water and cornflour to a smooth consistency, then pour into the roasting tin and add the crumbled stock cube. Bring to the boil, stirring well, then season to taste with salt and pepper. Serve piping hot with the carved lamb.

HERBED LAMB CHOPS

SERVES 4

This is the basic method for grilling first-cut lamb chops, also known as cutlets or rib chops.

1 tbsp extra virgin olive oil

1 garlic clove, halved

1 tsp each of dried basil and rosemary or 1 tbsp each of the chopped fresh herbs

1 tbsp lemon juice

black pepper

8 first-cut lamb chops 2cm /³/₄ in thick and trimmed of all but a thin layer of fat

sea salt

One hour before the chops are to be grilled, put the oil in a shallow dish wide enough to hold them in a single layer. Add the garlic, herbs and lemon juice. Grind a dusting of black pepper on both sides of the chops, then put them into the dish and turn to coat them with the oil. Leave for 1 hour, turning once or twice during this time, so that they are well and truly steeped in it.

15 minutes before serving time, heat the grill on high for 3 minutes. Arrange the chops on a rack in the grill pan. Put the pan 10cm/4in below the source of heat and grill the chops for 5 minutes on each side, or until they are a rich brown. Season with freshly ground sea salt.

VARIATION
Omit the basil and rosemary and use 1 tablespoon of tarragon mustard and 2 tablespoons of fresh tarragon (or 2 teaspoons of the dried herb) instead.

PATLICAN KEBABI

SERVES 6
KEEPS FOR 2 DAYS IN THE FRIDGE | FREEZES FOR 3 MONTHS

Lamb chops from the shoulder are meaty and flavourful, and though not quite tender enough to grill, they melt in the mouth when braised in a savoury sauce. This dish from Turkey uses for the sauce a most delicious combination of spices, which marries particularly well with the aubergine to make a really succulent dish for either a buffet or an informal dinner.

450g/1 lb aubergines

3½ tsp salt

6 lamb shoulder chops, about
175g/6oz each
in weight

5 grinds of black pepper

2 tbsp oil

1 onion, finely chopped

1 fat garlic clove, chopped

400ml/13½fl oz vegetable stock

2 tbsp tomato purée

2 tsp brown sugar

1 tsp ground cumin

1 tsp ground cinnamon

rice or bulgur, to serve

Cut the aubergines in 2.5cm/1 in cubes, then leave covered with water plus 3 teaspoons of salt for 30 minutes.

Meanwhile, lightly season the chops with salt and pepper, then in a large frying pan brown quickly on both sides in the oil. Lift out with a slotted spoon and drain on paper towels. In the same oil, cook the finely chopped onion over moderate heat until a rich golden brown, then add all the remaining ingredients except the aubergines, stir well and bring to the boil. Simmer, uncovered, for 5 minutes.

Preheat the oven to 150°C/300°F/Gas 2. Put the meat in an oven-to-table casserole, pour over the bubbling sauce, cover and cook in the slow oven for 1½ hours until very tender.

Meanwhile, squeeze as much moisture as possible from the aubergines and dry with paper towels. Deep-fry in 2 batches at 170°C/325°F (medium setting) for 5 minutes, then lift out on to paper towels. (If no deep-fryer is available, fry in 4 tablespoons oil in a covered frying pan for 10–15 minutes, or until soft and golden.) Add the fried aubergine to the casserole, re-cover and cook for a further 30 minutes. Serve from the casserole with rice or bulgur.

GREEK-JEWISH LAMB FRICASSÉE

SERVES 6–8
KEEPS FOR 3 DAYS IN THE FRIDGE | FREEZES FOR 3 MONTHS

This Graeco-Jewish casserole is by tradition cooked on top of the stove. If you're around the house, it's quite pleasant to do it this way, giving the pot a stir every now and again – it doesn't take more than 1 hour. If it's more convenient to cook it in the oven, it will take 1½–2 hours.

6 neck of lamb steaks, about 175g/6oz each, or 1.25kg/2½–3lb boned-out shoulder of lamb, cut into 3cm/1½in cubes

25g/1oz flour

1 tsp salt

15 grinds of black pepper

2 tbsp dried mint

3 tbsp olive oil

1 large onion, finely chopped

2 garlic cloves, finely chopped

225ml/8fl oz dry white wine, or chicken stock (see page 176) plus 1 tbsp lemon juice

2 tsp sugar

225g/8oz tiny button mushrooms

225g/8oz thin green beans, such as haricots verts or bobo beans

new potatoes or Basmati rice, to serve

Coat the lamb with flour seasoned with the salt, pepper and half the dried mint. Heat the oil and sauté the onion and garlic until a pale gold. Add the meat and sauté until a rich brown. Add the wine or chicken stock and lemon juice and bubble for 3 minutes to concentrate the flavour, then add the sugar and mushrooms.

Simmer for 1 hour on top of the stove or 1½ hours in a slow moderate oven, 170°C/325°F/Gas 3.

About 20 minutes before the end of the cooking time add the raw beans, stir well, and continue to cook until beans and meat are tender.

Serve with new potatoes cooked in their skins, or with Basmati rice flavoured as it cooks with 2 cardamom pods. The casserole reheats well.

VARIATION
Use 225g/8oz frozen peas instead of the beans, and add 10 minutes before the end of the cooking time.

KOFTA KEBABS
IN WARM PITTA BREAD

SERVES 6

Finely minced lamb seasoned with mint and spices and grilled on skewers, lamb kofta are popular throughout North Africa, the Balkans and the Middle East. Serve freshly cooked.

FOR THE KOFTA MEATBALLS

I small bunch of parsley (about 40g / I ½oz)

I garlic clove

675g/I ½lb lean minced lamb

I large thick slice (about 50g /2oz) white or brown bread, torn up

I onion, quartered

I ½ tsp dried mint

I tsp ground coriander

I tsp ground cumin

I tsp salt

10 grinds of black pepper

FOR THE SALAD

225g/8oz white cabbage

I carrot

I sweet red pepper

I tsp sweet chilli sauce

6 pitta breads

12 thinly sliced red onion rings

To make the kofta, put the parsley and garlic in the food processor and process until finely chopped. Add all the remaining ingredients, then pulse until the meat is finely chopped and the mixture just clings together. Knead well with the hands to make a smooth, plastic mixture. Shape it into 12 ovals, thread each onto a flat metal skewer, then squeeze firmly round the skewer until about 15cm/6in long and fairly flat. Chill for at least 2 hours, or overnight.

Shred the cabbage finely, grate the carrot coarsely and cut the pepper in fine strips, then mix all 3 together with the chilli sauce.

Cook the kebabs on a hot barbecue for about 10 minutes, turning frequently. Dip the pitta breads briefly into cold water and put on the barbecue for about 30 seconds on each side, or until puffed. Slit each bread open lengthways and spoon some of the salad inside. Slide the kebabs off the skewers and put 2 inside each pitta with a few onion rings.

DUTCH MEATBALLS WITH EGG AND LEMON SAUCE

SERVES 3–4
LEFTOVERS KEEP 24 HOURS IN THE FRIDGE | MEATBALLS AND STOCK (NOT SAUCE)
FREEZE FOR 3 MONTHS

FOR THE MEATBALLS

450g/1lb minced fresh veal

1 tbsp chopped parsley

1 onion, finely chopped

finely grated zest of
1 lemon

1 egg, beaten

½ tsp salt

pinch of white pepper

4 tbsp matzah meal or 25g/1oz
fresh breadcrumbs

FOR THE STEWING LIQUID

1 large onion, sliced

275ml/10fl oz/boiling water

½ tsp salt

1 pinch of white pepper

1 bay leaf

FOR THE SAUCE

2 tsp cornflour

5½ tbsp lemon juice

2 eggs

2 tsp sugar

225ml/8fl oz reserved stewing
liquid

Mix all the meatball ingredients together with a fork, then leave to stand for half an hour. Roll into balls the size of a walnut.

Bring the ingredients for the stewing liquid to the boil in an 20cm/8in saucepan, then add the meatballs – they should be barely covered by the liquid; if not, add a little extra boiling water. Bring to the boil, then reduce the heat until the liquid is barely bubbling. Cover and simmer for 45 minutes.

Discard the bay leaf, then lift out the meatballs and onion slices with a slotted spoon and set aside. Bubble the liquid until it is reduced to 225ml/8fl oz. Pour into a jug and rinse out the pan.

Put the cornflour into a bowl and gradually stir in the lemon juice, then whisk in the eggs, sugar and poaching liquid until smooth, or process for 10 seconds in a food processor.

Return to the pan and stir with a wooden spoon over low heat until the sauce thickens enough to coat the back of the spoon, then return the meatballs and onion slices to the pan and heat through until steaming – do not let it come to the boil or it may curdle. Taste and add a little more sugar if too acidic.

Alternatively, to cook the sauce in a microwave, mix the sauce ingredients in a microwave-safe jug. Cook on 30 per cent (300W) power for 2 minutes, stir well and cook for a further 2–3 minutes until thickened to coating consistency. Return to the pan, add the meatballs and onion slices and reheat until steaming.

FISH

'FRIED' FISH

SERVES 4

COOKED IN OIL KEEPS FOR 3 DAYS IN THE FRIDGE | FREEZES FOR 2 MONTHS

This baked recipe is a great way to serve hot 'fried' fish without being tied to the cooker or filling the house with the odour of hot oil. It also ensures that the very minimum of oil is absorbed.

125–175g /4–6oz breadcrumbs or matzah meal

4 fillets or steaks of any white fish

1 tsp salt

1 egg

50ml/2fl oz sunflower or vegetable oil or 25g/1oz melted butter

Put the crumbs or matzah meal in the oven to brown as it heats up, taking them out when they are well coloured.

Wash and salt the fish and leave to drain. Beat the egg with the fat and salt and put in a shallow casserole. Have ready a piece of greaseproof paper with the coating crumbs on it. Dry each piece of fish thoroughly with kitchen paper, then brush with the egg mixture and coat with the crumbs. Arrange the coated fish side by side on flat oven baking trays (no need to grease them). Leave in a cool place until required.

Preheat the oven to 200°C/400°F/Gas 6.

Put all the fish in the oven and allow to cook, without turning, for 20–25 minutes, depending on the thickness. Serve hot.

GEFILTE FISH PROVENÇALE

ALLOW 1–2 PATTIES PER SERVING
KEEPS FOR 4 DAYS IN THE FRIDGE

Gefilte fish was orginally a fish 'forcemeat' made from chopped or minced freshwater fish. Today, patties or balls of sea fish are poached in stock rather than stuffed into the fish. The patties in this recipe are poached in a delicious tomato and pepper sauce and can be served either warm or chilled.

GEFILTE FISH MIX (MAKES 12 PATTIES OR BALLS)

450g/1lb hake fillet, skinned, and 450g/1lb haddock fillet, skinned

1 onion, cut into 2.5cm/1in chunks

2 eggs

2 tsp salt, plus extra to salt the fish

1 pinch of white pepper

2 tsp sugar

1 tbsp oil

50g/2oz medium matzah meal

FOR THE SAUCE

1 tbsp olive oil

1 onion, finely chopped

425g/15oz passata or Italian tomatoes, puréed

2 tbsp tomato ketchup

1 orange or yellow pepper, seeded and thinly sliced

1 tsp salt

1 tsp brown sugar

10 grinds of black pepper

1 bay leaf

1/2 tsp dried Herbes de Provence

Wash and salt the fish and leave to drain. Put the onion in a food processor, together with the eggs, seasoning and oil, then process until reduced to a smooth purée. Pour this purée into a large bowl and stir in the matzah meal, then leave to swell.

Working in batches, process the fish in the food processor for 5 seconds until the fish is finely chopped, then add to the egg and onion purée and blend in using a large fork. Repeat until all the fish has been processed, then mix thoroughly. The mixture should be firm enough to shape into a soft patty. If it feels too 'cloggy', add 1 or 2 tablespoons of water and stir. If it feels very soft, stir in 1 or 2 tablespoons of the matzah meal. Leave for half an hour, or overnight in the fridge if preferred. The gefilte fish mix is now ready to shape.

Preheat the oven to 300°F/150°C/Gas 2. Mould the fish mixture with wet hands into oval patties, each about 7cm/2½in long, 4cm/1½in wide and 2cm/¾in thick. Cover and set aside.

To make the sauce, heat the oil and sauté the onion until soft and transparent, then add all the remaining ingredients and bubble until reduced to a thick coating consistency.

Arrange the fish patties in a shallow ovenproof dish, pour over the sauce and loosely cover with foil. Bake for 1 hour basting the patties once or twice with the sauce. Serve warm or chilled.

GRILLED HERRINGS
WITH FRESH APPLE SAUCE

SERVES 4
LEFTOVERS AND SAUCE KEEP FOR 4 DAYS IN THE FRIDGE | SAUCE FREEZES
FOR 3 MONTHS

Fine, fat fillets of fresh herring grilled until the flesh is creamy and firm in texture make a wonderful mid-week meal. The piquant sauce helps to neutralize the natural oiliness of this most nourishing of fish. As they have special seasons when they are in their prime, consult the fishmonger before you buy.

4–6 fresh herring fillets cut from a 350–450g/12–14oz fish

FOR THE SAUCE

nut of butter or margarine

350g/12oz Bramley (cooking) apples, or Granny Smiths, peeled, cored and roughly chopped

1 tbsp brown sugar

2 tsp water

3 tsp creamed horseradish

FOR THE TOPPING

2½ tbsp sunflower oil

4 tsp cider vinegar or red wine vinegar

3 tsp Dijon mustard

2 tsp Worcestershire Sauce

1 tsp light soy sauce

½ tsp sea salt

15 grinds of black pepper

First, make the sauce by melting the butter in a small pan and adding the apple, sugar and water. Cover and simmer gently until the apples are very soft, then beat to a purée with a wooden spoon, stick blender or food processor. Stir in the creamed horseradish.

Wash the fish, salt lightly and leave in a colander to drain for 10 minutes.

Meanwhile, mix the topping ingredients together in a small bowl.

Lightly grease the grill pan and heat it up 7.5cm/3in from the grill for 3 minutes. Then lay the fish fillets in it side by side, skin-side down, and brush them thickly with the topping mixture. Grill for 10 minutes until the fish is a rich brown. Serve at once, accompanied by the apple sauce at room temperature.

GOLDEN FILLETS OF MACKEREL WITH A CLEMENTINE AND CUCUMBER SALAD

SERVES 6
LEFTOVERS KEEP FOR 2 DAYS IN THE FRIDGE | DO NOT FREEZE

This is a fish dish to choose if you're looking for a rich taste and satisfying texture without a stratospheric price. Mackerel has a high oil content, and though this is excellent from a health point of view, it does need to be tempered by some kind of acidity, provided in this recipe by the tangy salad and delicious marinade that accompanies it.

6 split mackerel fillets cut from 3 whole fish (each 350–400g/ 12–14 oz)

sea salt

FOR THE MARINADE

2 tbsp light soy sauce

2 tbsp fresh orange juice

1 tbsp sun-dried tomato purée or tomato purée

1 tbsp chopped parsley

1 garlic clove, chopped

2 tsp Worcestershire sauce

2 tsp lemon juice

15 grinds of black pepper

FOR THE SALAD

3 tbsp sugar or granular sweetener

3 tbsp boiling water

5 tbsp cider vinegar

4 tbsp chopped dill

10 grinds of black pepper

1 cucumber, thinly sliced

6 clementines

Wash and lightly salt the mackerel fillets, then lay side by side in a heatproof dish suitable for grilling. Mix together the marinade ingredients, then spoon or brush over the fish in an even layer. Allow to marinate at room temperature for 1 hour.

To make the salad, put the sugar or sweetener in a small bowl, add the boiling water and stir until dissolved. Then stir in the vinegar, dill and black pepper. Pour over the thinly sliced cucumber and the peeled and sectioned clementines in a shallow dish and leave for at least 1 hour. Serve with the fish.

Grill 10cm/4in from a hot grill for 9–10 minutes, or until the fish flakes easily and is firm to the touch.

I like to serve this dish with crispy jacket potatoes – they take less than 30 minutes if you have a combination microwave. The grilled fish is equally delicious served at room temperature as part of a cold buffet.

POACHED SALMON 3 WAYS

TO POACH A SALMON FILLET

KEEPS FOR 3 DAYS IN THE FRIDGE | FREEZES FOR 3 MONTHS

Place the washed and salted fish on a double piece of parchment paper or foil greased with a little oil, then fold into a parcel, securing it, if necessary, with loosely tied string. Put it in a pan and cover with cold water. Add 2 teaspoons salt and a speck of pepper and bring slowly to the boil.

To serve hot Reduce the heat and allow to simmer (but never boil) for 6 minutes for each 450g/1 lb and 6 minutes extra. Lift out, drain well, unwrap and serve.

To serve cold When the water comes to the boil bubble for 3 minutes only, then remove from the heat and leave the fish in the covered pan until the liquid is cold – at least 3 hours. It can be kept in the liquid for up to 3 days in the fridge.

TO POACH SALMON STEAKS ON THE STOVE

Lightly butter a large frying pan. Lay the salmon steaks on the pan and add 175ml/6fl oz water or fish stock for 4 steaks, 350ml/12fl oz for 8 steaks. Bring to simmering point, cover and simmer – never boil – for 10 minutes, turning the fish once.

TO POACH SALMON STEAKS IN THE MICROWAVE

SERVES 4
KEEPS FOR 3 DAYS IN THE FRIDGE | LEFTOVERS FREEZE FOR 3 MONTHS

4 salmon steaks, about 175g/6oz each

150ml/5fl oz fish stock

squeeze of lemon juice

salt

white pepper

Arrange the washed steaks round the edge of a round microwave-safe dish, with the thin part of the steaks to the centre. Pour on the stock and lemon juice and cover, then cook on 60 per cent (600W) power for 6 minutes, turning the fish over after 3 minutes. Leave to stand for 5 minutes, then sprinkle lightly with salt and pepper.

FILLETS OF SALMON UNDER A CRUSHED PECAN CRUST

SERVES 6
SERVE THE SAME DAY

750g/1²/₃lb thick salmon fillet, cut into 6–8 pieces

salt

white pepper

2 tbsp reduced-calorie mayonnaise

FOR THE CRUST

185g/6½oz shelled pecans

4 tbsp snipped chives

2 tbsp unsalted butter, melted

In the food processor, pulse the nuts until coarsely ground, then mix with the chives and melted butter in a small bowl. Lightly grease with butter a shallow tin wide enough to hold the pieces of salmon in one layer. Arrange them in this dish and season lightly with the salt and pepper, then spread the surface with a thin layer of mayonnaise and cover completely with the nut mixture, patting it on well. Leave until shortly before serving.

About 15 minutes before serving, preheat the oven to 220°C/425°F/Gas 7. Put the salmon in the oven for 8–10 minutes, or until the salmon flakes easily with a fork. Keep warm until required.

SALMON KEDGEREE

SERVES 4
KEEPS FOR 2 DAYS IN THE FRIDGE | DO NOT FREEZE

A delicious variation of the classic recipe, this can be served as a main or as a starter for 6 before a light meat-based main course.

I tbsp sunflower or vegetable oil

I shallot or I small bunch of spring onion bulbs, finely chopped

225g/8oz Basmati rice

5½ tbsp dry white wine (optional)

575ml/I pint fish stock, or 575ml/ I pint water plus I fish stock cube

I tbsp lemon juice

½ tsp salt

8 grinds of black pepper

225g/8oz raw salmon fillet, skinned

4 hard-boiled eggs, shelled and roughly chopped or quartered

25g/I oz/2 tbsp butter or margarine

I tbsp chopped parsley

25g/I oz flaked almonds

In an 20cm/8in lidded frying pan, heat the oil and fry the onion until very soft and creamy gold in colour, then add the rice and toss over a high heat for I minute. Add the wine (if using) and bubble until it has almost evaporated, then add the stock, lemon juice, salt and pepper, and bring to the boil. Cover tightly and simmer gently for 15–20 minutes until the rice is bite-tender (taste it).

Cut the salmon into I cm/½in chunks and add to the rice, cover and cook for a further 5 minutes, stirring occasionally, over gentle heat until the fish is cooked. Stir in the chopped egg (reserving some to garnish), butter or margarine and parsley, and mix with a fork. Turn into a heatproof serving dish and sprinkle with the almonds. Just before serving, pop under a hot grill for 2 minutes until golden brown, then garnish with the egg.

SAMAK KEBAB

SERVES 6
KEEPS FOR 1 DAY IN THE FRIDGE | DO NOT FREEZE

For this recipe I have borrowed a Turkish way of marinating cubes of fish in a spicy sauce. The marinade softens the texture of the fish, while the spices add extra zing. Kebabs prepared by this method are best hot off the grill or barbecue, but they're still delicious eaten at room temperature up to an hour after cooking.

900g/2lb thick fillets of firm white fish (halibut, sea bass, haddock or cod), skinned

4 tbsp olive oil

FOR THE MARINADE

2 large onions

8 tbsp lemon juice

2 tsp ground cumin

2 fat garlic cloves, finely chopped

1 tsp paprika

1 tsp sea salt

20 grinds of black pepper

TO SERVE

coarsely chopped parsley

lemon wedges

paprika

Basmati rice

Cut the fish into 2.5cm/1 in cubes and put in one layer in a shallow dish.

To make the marinade, peel, grate and extract the juice from the onions by pressing them through a sieve into a small bowl. Mix the onion juice together with the remaining marinade ingredients in a small bowl. (Reserve the grated onion for another use.) Pour the marinade over fish. Leave for at least an hour, turning 2–3 times.

Thread the fish on to metal or soaked wooden skewers and brush all over with the olive oil. The dish can be prepared to this stage early in the day. To cook, grill or barbecue for 6–8 minutes until golden, turning frequently.

To serve, sprinkle the coarsely chopped parsley on an oval fish platter, lay the fish on top and garnish with the lemon wedges and a dusting of paprika. Serve with rice or potatoes and a mixed salad.

GRILLED TROUT
WITH SESAME SAUCE

SERVES 4

4 whole trout weighing between
225–350g/8–12oz each

a little oil

SESAME SAUCE FOR TROUT

2 tbsp butter

1 tbsp sesame oil

2 tbsp white sesame seeds

4 tbsp fresh lemon juice

100ml/3½fl oz fish or vegetable
stock

1 pinch of salt

1 small pinch of white pepper

Have the fish gutted and cleaned but leave the head on (this keeps it moist). Brush the skin lightly with oil. Grill the fish under a moderate heat for 5–10 minutes each side, depending on the thickness (a fish 4cm/1½in thick will take 15–18 minutes in total). Test by removing a little skin and see if the fish flakes easily with a fork.

In a small saucepan, melt the butter or margarine and sesame oil, then add the sesame seeds and sauté gently until they are golden brown, tossing them in the pan several times. Add the remaining ingredients and bring to the boil, then simmer until the liquid is reduced by half. When the fish are cooked, transfer to individual plates and remove the skin. Reheat the sauce and spoon over the fish. Serve at once.

VEGETABLE DISHES AND SIDES

ISRAELI FRUITED WINTER SALAD

SERVES 6 | SERVE THE SAME DAY

A refreshing green salad to serve either as a starter or for a buffet supper.

50g/2oz blanched split almonds

½ iceberg lettuce, shredded

10cm/4in piece of Chinese leaf (Napa cabbage), finely sliced, or any preferred salad greens

175g/6oz seedless black grapes

FOR THE DRESSING

75ml/3fl oz sunflower oil

2 tbsp extra virgin olive oil

1 tbsp red wine vinegar or raspberry vinegar

1 tbsp fresh lemon juice

1 tsp caster sugar

½ tsp wholegrain mustard

½ tsp sea salt

8 grinds of black pepper

Shake all the dressing ingredients together in a screw-top jar until slightly thickened, then chill for several hours.

Toast and lightly salt the blanched almonds.

Arrange the finely shredded lettuce and Chinese leaves or other greens in a wide salad bowl, cover and chill. Shortly before serving, add the halved grapes and the almonds and toss with the dressing.

ISRAELI SALAD

SERVES 6
SERVE THE SAME DAY

This is the archetypal kibbutz salad, served in Israel at breakfast, lunch and dinner! Whether it's prepared for 200 kibbutzniks or by street vendors who spoon it into your pitta bread along with their freshly fried falafel balls, it's always made with diced vegetables – cucumber, tomato and sweet peppers, cut large or small, according to the patience of the cook. This makes a refreshing foil for grilled dishes, whether meat or fish, but it's equally good with cold poultry and meats.

I red pepper

I green pepper

I cucumber, unpeeled

3 large firm, preferably vine-ripened, tomatoes

coarse salt

FOR THE DRESSING

4 tbsp sunflower oil

I tbsp fruity olive oil

I tbsp wine vinegar

I tbsp lemon juice

I fat garlic clove, crushed

I tsp salt

10 grinds of black pepper

I tsp caster sugar

I tbsp finely snipped fresh mint or I tsp dried mint

2 tbsp chopped parsley

All the salad ingredients and the dressing can be prepared up to a day ahead, if you wish, but it is best to combine them an hour before serving to retain the characteristic crispness.

Halve and deseed the peppers and remove the white pith. Cut each of the vegetables into even 2cm/¾in cubes or squares, then put the tomatoes and peppers into separate bowls, cover and chill. Put the cucumber cubes into a salad spinner or sieve, sprinkle with I teaspoon of coarse salt and leave for 30 minutes, then spin or drain and refrigerate.

In a screw-top jar, shake together all the dressing ingredients except the fresh herbs. Add the dried mint, if using, then leave for several hours to mature in flavour. Put the cucumber, pepper and tomato cubes into a large bowl, then stir in the chopped parsley and mint, together with the dressing, and mix well, using 2 spoons. Arrange the salad in a fairly shallow dish – it looks particularly effective against black or white. Serve cool but not chilled.

HUNGARIAN CUCUMBER SALAD

SERVES 6
KEEPS FOR 2 DAYS IN THE FRIDGE | DO NOT FREEZE

An excellent salad for a low-fat diet, as no oil is used in the dressing. Although not traditional, the salad looks pretty with a mixture of baby red and yellow tomatoes.

1 cucumber

350g/12oz small tomatoes

1 large red pepper

3 tsp cooking (kosher) salt

FOR THE DRESSING

2 tsp caster sugar
or granular sweetener

1 tbsp hot water

4 tbsp wine vinegar

15 grinds of black pepper

1 tsp salt

1 tbsp fresh snipped dill, chives
or chopped mint

Make the salad at least 2 or 3 hours before serving to allow the flavour to develop. Slice the cucumber as thinly as possible. Cut the tomatoes in halves or quarters according to size. Halve, deseed and remove the white pith from the pepper, then cut the flesh in thin strips. Put the cucumber slices and tomatoes in a bowl, sprinkle with cooking salt and leave for an hour.

Put the sugar in a bowl, pour on the hot water, stir well, then add all the remaining dressing ingredients. (If using granular sweetener, dissolve in cold water.)

Lift out the tomatoes and cucumber slices with a slotted spoon and discard the liquid that has come out of them, then return them to the bowl and add to the peppers. Pour the dressing over the vegetables and toss them together gently. Turn into a serving dish and chill until required.

KATSIS KISHUIM

SERVES 4–6 AS A STARTER, 6–8 AS A DIP.
KEEPS FOR 3 DAYS IN THE FRIDGE | DO NOT FREEZE

This Israeli courgette pâté is light on the tongue, with a delicate but intriguing flavour – no one can guess the main ingredient without asking. It makes an excellent vegetarian alternative to chopped liver.

2 tbsp butter

1 small onion, thinly sliced

500g/1lb 2oz courgettes, topped, tailed and thinly sliced

½ tsp fine sea salt

8 grinds of black pepper

1 pinch of Cayenne pepper or hot chilli powder

1 sprig of parsley

2 hard-boiled eggs, shelled and quartered

Melt the butter and sauté the onion over a moderate heat until it has turned a rich gold, then add the courgettes and seasonings and toss well. When the courgettes begin to colour, cover and steam them over a low heat, shaking the pan occasionally until they feel tender when pierced with a sharp knife – 5–6 minutes.

Chop the parsley in a food processor, then add the hard-boiled egg quarters with the vegetables and juices and process until the mixture becomes a smooth pâté. Turn into a terrine or pottery bowl, cover and chill for several hours, then leave at room temperature for half an hour before serving.

AVOCADO AND EGG PÂTÉ

SERVES 4 AS A PÂTÉ, 6 AS A DIP
KEEPS FOR 2 DAYS IN THE FRIDGE | DO NOT FREEZE

Another favourite Israeli starter. There is a strong affinity with the egg and spring onion forspeise (see page 23), but this has the added richness of avocados to give it a different flavour and texture.

½ large bunch of parsley

½ small bunch of spring onion (scallion) bulbs

2 ripe avocados

1 tbsp lemon juice

2 hard-boiled eggs, shelled and halved

1 tsp fine sea salt

5 grinds of black pepper

1 tbsp mayonnaise

crisps, crackers or challah, to serve

Chop the parsley and the spring onions finely in a food processor. Add the peeled, pitted and roughly cubed avocados and the lemon juice, then add the eggs and seasonings. Pulse until the eggs are finely chopped. Turn into a bowl and add enough of the mayonnaise to bind the mixture into a pâté. Taste and re-season if necessary. Pile into a shallow bowl and chill until required. Serve with crisps, crackers or spread on fingers of challah.

CAPONATA ALLA SICILIANA

SERVES 6
KEEPS FOR 3 DAYS IN THE FRIDGE | DO NOT FREEZE

According to the Sicilian cookery book *Sicilia e le Isole in bocca*, this rich and wonderful aubergine stew – a culinary relative of French ratatouille – originated in the Mafia port of Palermo. Serve with plenty of brown or rye country bread to mop up the delicious juices.

I heaped tbsp salt

900g/2lb fine aubergines, unpeeled and cut into 2cm/¾in cubes

125ml/4fl oz olive oil

2 garlic cloves, finely chopped

5 tbsp extra virgin olive oil

2 onions, finely sliced

I celery heart (6–8 stalks), sliced I cm/½ in thick

425g/15oz canned chopped tomatoes, well drained

225g/8oz large black olives, pitted and sliced

2 tbsp capers in brine, well drained

2 tbsp granulated sugar or granular sweetener

4 tbsp white wine vinegar

15 grinds of black pepper

I tsp freeze-dried basil

TO SERVE

tiny sprigs or leaves of fresh herbs – coriander, parsley or basil

Half-fill a salad spinner with cold water, add the salt and then the aubergines, cover and leave for 30 minutes. Pour off the water, then spin dry.

Heat the oil in a large lidded sauté pan, add the well-dried aubergines and the garlic, toss to coat with the fat and cover. Allow to brown and to soften for 20 minutes, stirring 2 or 3 times. Remove with a slotted spoon.

Meanwhile, heat the 5 tablespoons of extra virgin oil in an 20cm/8in pan, put in the onions, stir well, cover and cook gently until golden and softened. Add the celery and cook for a further 5 minutes, then add all the remaining ingredients except the aubergines and cook, uncovered, until thick and juicy.

Stir in the sautéed aubergines, tossing carefully to mix all the ingredients thoroughly. Chill for several hours, or overnight. Season with sea salt and freshly ground black pepper, then sprinkle with the herbs before serving.

OMELETTE BASQUAISE

SERVES 4

4 tbsp butter

2 tsp olive oil

1 small onion, finely chopped

1 red pepper, deseeded and diced

2 mushrooms, sliced

3 canned or fresh tomatoes, chopped

1 small garlic clove, crushed

1 tsp dried oregano

1 tsp chopped parsley

salt and black pepper

6 eggs, beaten with ½ tsp salt and 8 grinds of black pepper

50g/2oz mature Cheddar, grated

Melt the butter with the oil in an 20cm/8in omelette pan, then add the onion. Sauté gently for 5 minutes, then add the pepper, mushrooms, tomatoes, garlic and seasonings.

Cover and cook for 10 minutes until soft, then uncover and pour on the eggs. Stir well, then cook until set and golden brown underneath. Sprinkle with the grated cheese, then place the pan very briefly under a hot grill until the top is melted and golden. Serve at once from the dish.

BADINJAN KUKU
PERSIAN AUBERGINE FRITATTA

SERVES 4

2 aubergines

salt

4 tbsp extra virgin olive oil

I large beefsteak tomato, finely sliced

I small onion, finely chopped

I garlic clove, finely chopped

2½ tbsp finely chopped fresh dill or parsley

2½ tbsp raisins

pinch of ground saffron (optional)

10 grinds of black pepper

I tsp salt

6 large eggs, beaten

Cut the aubergines into roughly 2.5cm/I in chunks, put on a large plate or in a salad spinner and sprinkle liberally with salt. After 30 minutes, rinse well with cold water, drain thoroughly and dry (this reduces the amount of oil needed for frying).

Heat the oil in a large frying pan, add the well-dried aubergine chunks, the tomato, onion and garlic, and sauté gently for 5 minutes. Stir in the dill, raisins, saffron, black pepper and salt.

Pour on the eggs. Stir well, then cook until set and golden brown underneath. If you like, place the pan very briefly under a hot grill until the top is set and golden. Serve at once from the dish.

PIPERRADA

SERVES 4
SERVE HOT OFF THE PAN

Though capsicums are native to Mexico and Central America, they have been a mainstay of Sephardi and Ashkenazi cuisine for centuries. A point of interest: weight for weight, peppers contain between 6 and 9 times the Vitamin C of tomatoes, and contain only 78 calories per 100g/3½oz – the weight of an average pepper.

5 tbsp extra virgin olive oil

2 onions, thinly sliced

2 garlic cloves, finely chopped

2 large, very ripe beefsteak tomatoes, halved, deseeded and sectioned

2 yellow peppers, deseeded and cut into thin strips

2 red peppers, deseeded and cut into thin strips

sea salt

black pepper

6 eggs

Heat the oil in a large lidded frying pan. Add the onions and garlic and sauté, covered until softened and golden. Add the tomatoes and peppers to the pan and simmer gently, uncovered, for 10–12 minutes until the peppers are softened but still slightly firm. Uncover, reduce the heat and season to taste.

Beat the eggs just to blend, then pour over the pepper mixture. Cook very gently for several minutes, or long enough for the eggs to begin to set but still be very creamy. Slide on to a warm serving dish.

Preheat the oven to 160°C/325°F/Gas 3 and oil a gratin dish or ovenproof pan (about 25cm/10in in diameter). Stir the vegetable mixture into the eggs, turn into the baking dish and cook, uncovered, for 35–40 minutes, or until firm to gentle touch. Leave to cool for a couple of minutes before cutting. Serve at once.

IMAM BAYELDI

SERVES 6
KEEPS FOR 3 DAYS IN THE FRIDGE | DO NOT FREEZE

The following recipe is how the Turks make this rich, luscious baked aubergine dish, though different versions are served all over the Middle East.

6 small, oval aubergines, each weighing about 225g/8oz

2 large onions

3 tbsp extra virgin olive oil

whole tomatoes, drained from a 425g/15oz can, chopped

2 tbsp currants

1/2 tsp ground cinnamon

1/2 tsp ground cumin

1 tsp brown sugar

1/2 tsp salt

10 grinds of black pepper

3 tbsp chopped parsley

FOR THE SAUCE

125ml/4fl oz hot water

4 tbsp extra virgin olive oil

2 1/2 tbsp lemon juice

2 tsp brown sugar

1 garlic clove, halved

TO SERVE

crusty bread or warm pitta bread

Cut a deep slit lengthways in the centre of each aubergine, sprinkle inside with salt and leave for 30 minutes. Squeeze out any black juices, rinse under cold water and pat dry.

Slice the onions finely, then sauté gently in the olive oil until soft and golden. Add the tomatoes, currants, spices, sugar, salt and pepper and simmer gently until the mixture is thick but still juicy. Add the parsley.

Cool, then use to stuff the slits in each aubergine. Arrange side by side in a shallow casserole, slit-side up, and add the sauce ingredients – first the water and olive oil, then pour over the lemon juice and sprinkle with the sugar. Add the garlic.

Cover the dish and simmer very gently, either on top of the stove or in the oven at 160°C/325°F/Gas 3, for 1 1/2 hours, or until quite soft and most of the liquid has been absorbed. Chill, preferably overnight.

When you are ready, lift the aubergines from the sauce, spoon a little sauce over each one, and serve at room temperature with crusty bread or warm pitta.

EGYPTIAN-JEWISH STUFFED AUBERGINES

SERVES 6
KEEPS FOR 3 DAYS IN THE FRIDGE | FREEZES FOR 3 MONTHS

This is the way Egyptian Jews prepare stuffed aubergines. It is one of my favourite stuffed vegetable recipes. The dish reheats well.

3 glossy boat-shaped aubergines, each weighing about 225g /8oz, or 6 long slender ones

5½ tbsp sunflower or other flavourless oil for frying (add extra if required)

flour, for coating

FOR THE STUFFING

450g/1 lb raw minced beef

1 egg, beaten

1 tsp salt

10 grinds of black pepper

1 tsp paprika

5 tbsp uncooked rice

fried aubergine flesh (see below)

FOR THE SAUCE

½ onion, finely chopped

400g/14oz canned Italian tomatoes, strained, or 400g/14oz passata

4 tbsp brown sugar

juice of 1 large lemon (3 tbsp)

½ tsp salt

1 pinch of white pepper

a little chicken stock or water if necessary

Preheat the oven to 180°C/350°F/Gas 4. Cut the aubergines in half and scoop out the flesh, leaving a good 5mm/¼in of aubergine all the way round. Roughly chop the scooped-out aubergine flesh, then fry until soft in a little oil. Add to the meat, together with all the remaining stuffing ingredients, and mix well. Mound the meat mixture into each aubergine, pressing it in firmly.

Dip each stuffed aubergine in flour, then brown it quickly on both sides in a little hot oil. Arrange the browned aubergines in a wide ovenproof casserole.

Start the sauce in the same oil. Cook the chopped onion, covered, until soft and golden brown, then stir in all the remaining ingredients for the sauce. When the sauce is bubbling, pour it round the aubergines – they should be just submerged. If not, top up with a little chicken stock or water.

Cover the casserole and put in the oven for half an hour until the sauce is bubbling nicely, then turn the oven down to 150°C/300°F/Gas 2 and cook for a further 2 hours. When the aubergines are ready, they will have absorbed most of the sauce, leaving just enough to pour over each aubergine when it is served.

FRITADA DE ESPINACA
SEPHARDI SPINACH AND MUSHROOM BAKE

SERVES 4–5 AS A MAIN DISH | EAT WARM OR AT ROOM TEMPERATURE
KEEPS FOR 2 DAYS IN THE FRIDGE | DO NOT FREEZE

This baked omelette is especially creamy in texture as it is made with a herb or garlic and herb cream cheese. It can be frozen uncooked. Thaw and bake when required. If you have the option, bake on a conventional rather than a forced air (convection) oven setting so the bake is moist and succulent.

225g/8oz pack frozen leaf spinach, thawed

25g/1oz/2 tbsp butter or margarine

the bulbs and 7.5cm/3in of stalk from a small bunch of spring onions, finely sliced

125g/4oz mushrooms, finely sliced

3 eggs

about 150g/5oz herb cream cheese

175g/6oz grated Lancashire or Cheddar cheese (reserve 4 tbsp for topping)

1 tsp salt

15 grinds of black pepper

1 tbsp chopped parsley

Preheat the oven to 190°C/375°F/Gas 5. Grease a rectangular baking dish about 28 x 18cm/11 x 7in and about 7cm/3in deep, or a foil container 20–22cm/8–9in square and about 7cm/3in deep.

Put the spinach in a sieve and press out as much moisture as possible, then roughly chop. Heat the butter in a sauté pan and sauté the onions, covered, until soft and golden. Add the mushrooms and cook over a brisk heat until softened and golden brown. Add the spinach and continue to cook, stirring, until there is no free moisture in the pan – this will take 2–3 minutes.

Whisk the eggs in a small bowl. Put the cream cheese in a larger bowl and stir in the grated cheese. Add the eggs, sautéed vegetables and seasonings.

Pour into the prepared dish and scatter with the reserved cheese. Bake for 25–30 minutes, or until firm to the touch and golden brown.

PASTA WITH A
SYRACUSE SAUCE

SERVES 4

KEEPS FOR 3 DAYS IN THE FRIDGE | SAUCE OR LEFTOVERS FREEZE FOR 1 MONTH

The joy of pasta is that it takes so little time to cook, and this dish looks particularly inviting made with a mixture of the three colours of pasta spirals. Anchovies are always used in Sicily, but if you prefer the sauce to be wholly vegetarian a tablespoon of drained capers can be added instead. It is traditionally served with flavourful grated cheese such as Pecorino.

350g/12oz rigatoni or penne pasta

finely grated cheese

FOR THE SAUCE

450g/1lb aubergines, cut into 1cm/½in cubes

1 red pepper

1 yellow pepper

1 tbsp sunflower or vegetable oil

1 tbsp olive oil

2 garlic cloves, finely chopped

425g/15oz canned chopped Italian tomatoes

12 fat black olives, pitted

50g/2oz canned anchovies, drained and cut into 1cm/½in lengths

10 grinds of black pepper

6 basil leaves, coarsely shredded

First, start the sauce. Put the unpeeled cubes of aubergine in a salad spinner or colander and sprinkle thickly with salt. Leave for 30 minutes, then rinse well and dry.

Meanwhile, grill the peppers until the skin looks charred, leave wrapped in paper towels for 5 minutes, then strip off the skin with your fingers and cut the flesh in narrow strips.

In a heavy 23cm/9in saucepan or deep lidded frying pan, heat the oils and sauté the aubergine, covered, for 10 minutes, then uncover and add all the remaining ingredients. Cover and simmer gently for 5 minutes, then taste and add a little salt if necessary. The sauce should be thick but juicy.

Meanwhile, cook the pasta according to the packet directions, then drain well. Put the hot sauce into a bowl and, using 2 spoons, toss with the hot pasta so that every piece is coated before turning into a warm dish. Serve at once with the grated cheese.

UNCOOKED PASTA SAUCES

In these two pasta dishes, the sauce is not cooked. To prepare the first, all you need is a food processor, and for the second, a sharp cook's knife. But because the sauce is only at room temperature, it's essential to have the serving dish and plates very hot, so that the pasta doesn't become lukewarm when it is mixed with the sauce.

SPAGHETTINI WITH BLACK OLIVES

SERVES 2
MAKE AND EAT THE SAME DAY

150g/5oz spaghettini or spaghetti

150g/5oz fat black olives

1 garlic clove

1 tsp finely chopped oregano, or ¼ tsp dried

4 tbsp extra virgin olive oil

10 grinds of black pepper

1 tbsp unsalted butter

First cook the pasta in boiling salted water until al dente according to the packet directions. While it cooks, cut the olive flesh away from the pit and chop coarsely with a knife. Chop the garlic and herbs finely, then put with the olives in a small bowl. Slowly stir in the olive oil and add the pepper. Melt the butter in a large bowl in the microwave. Drain the pasta (leaving some water clinging to it), then add to the butter. Toss well to coat the strands, then add the olive mixture. Toss together and serve.

LINGUINE WITH WALNUT SAUCE

SERVES 6
MAKE AND EAT THE SAME DAY

400g/14 oz fresh linguine

75g/3oz freshly grated Parmesan

FOR THE SAUCE

125g/4oz shelled walnuts

½ small garlic clove, peeled

4 tbsp butter

100ml/3½fl oz fromage frais

½ tsp salt

15 grinds of black pepper

Make the sauce in a food processor. Blend the walnuts, garlic, butter, fromage frais, salt and pepper very thoroughly until you have a smooth sauce.

Cook the pasta according to the packet directions. Reserve 4 tablespoons of the cooking liquid, then drain the pasta lightly in a colander. Add the reserved liquid to the sauce to thin it to coating consistency, then mix it with the pasta. Add the grated Parmesan, toss well together and serve.

SAUTÉED SWEET PEPPERS

SERVES 4
EAT HOT OFF THE PAN

The capsicum or sweet pepper needs sun and warmth to mature and sweeten it. Whatever the colour, the vegetable should be glossy and firm and quite free from bruises. Before it is used, every scrap of the white ribs and bitter seeds needs to be discarded. This is the simplest – and one of the most delicious – ways to cook peppers.

4 large glossy peppers of any colour

2½ tbsp extra virgin olive oil

1 small garlic clove, crushed with salt

1 tbsp chopped oregano, or 1 tsp dried marjoram or oregano

1 tsp salt

Cut the peppers in half and remove the seeds and ribs. Wash and then slice in strips, 3 to each half. Heat the oil gently, then add the peppers and cook quickly for a few minutes until beginning to soften, stirring frequently. Add the garlic, cover, reduce the heat to the minimum and cook slowly for 15–20 minutes until tender. Add the herbs and seasonings.

These are best eaten hot off the pan, as they tend to go soggy if reheated.

VIENNESE BRAISED RED CABBAGE

SERVES 6–8

KEEPS FOR 4 DAYS IN THE FRIDGE | FREEZES FOR 3 MONTHS

Jewish cooks with a German and Austrian background make wonderful variations on the theme of red cabbage, using apples, dried fruit, fruit jelly, vinegar and wine in different permutations to create the sweet and sour effect that's characteristic of this luscious dish.

900g/2lb red cabbage

50g/2oz butter

1 large onion, finely chopped

2 tbsp brown sugar (optional)

3½ tbsp crab apple or redcurrant jelly

3 tbsp cider vinegar

1 tbsp water

2 tsp salt

¼ tsp white pepper

1 large bay leaf

Preheat the oven to 190°C/375°F/Gas 5.

Quarter the cabbage, remove and discard the stalk section, then shred finely by hand or in a food processor. Rinse in cold water and drain well.

Melt the butter in a heavy pan large enough to hold the cabbage. Add the finely chopped onion and cook for 5 minutes until golden brown. Add the sugar if dusing, and stir until it begins to caramelize. Now add the cabbage and all the remaining ingredients, stirring well to blend until bubbling. Transfer to an oven casserole – a covered roaster or an enamelled steel dish are both excellent.

Cook in the oven for 45 minutes to 1 hour. Stir twice. Taste and add more sugar if necessary – the cabbage should have an equal balance of sour and sweet. It should also have a little bite left when it is ready. It can then be kept hot at 140°C/275°F/Gas 1 for as long as required. It also reheats extremely well, covered, in the microwave on 100 per cent (1000W) power for 2½ minutes or until steaming.

POTATO LATKES

Latkes are fritters that were originally made with cream cheese in honour of Judith, whose heroism is said to have inspired the Maccabees in their rebellion. As Chanukkah falls in December, when fresh milk was scarce, the Jews of Eastern Europe substituted potatoes for cheese.

4 large potatoes, peeled, weight about 675g/1 ½lb – enough to fill a 575ml/1 pint measure when grated

½ onion, either cut into 2.5cm/1in chunks (food processor method) or finely sliced (traditional method)

2 eggs

1 tsp salt

speck of white pepper

4½ tbsp self-raising flour or 4½ tbsp plain flour plus a pinch of baking powder

any flavourless oil, such as sunflower, for frying

Only grate the potatoes 15 minutes before cooking to avoid them turning brown.

Traditional method Grate the potatoes almost to a pulp. Leave in a sieve to drain for 10 minutes. Put in a bowl and add the remaining ingredients.

In a large heavy frying pan, put enough oil to come to a depth of 1cm/½in. When the oil is hot (190°C/375°F), put in tablespoons of mixture, flattening each latke with the back of the spoon. Cook over steady moderate heat for 5 minutes on each side until a rich brown. Drain on crumpled kitchen paper, then serve as soon as possible, or keep hot in a moderate oven, 180°C/350°F/Gas 4, for up to 15 minutes.

Food processor method With some food processor grating discs, the potato pulp will be too coarse, so you may need to pulse briefly after grating, using the metal blade. If you have a fine shredding disk or prefer more rösti-like latkes, omit this stage.

Cut the potatoes to fit the feed tube, then grate through the grating disc. Turn into a metal sieve and press down firmly with a spoon to remove as much moisture as possible. Leave to drain.

Put the onion, eggs, seasonings and flour into the bowl and process with the metal blade until smooth – about 5 seconds. Add the drained potatoes and pulse for 3–4 seconds until the potatoes are finer and are almost reduced to a coarse pulp. Shape and fry as in the traditional method.

SWEETCORN FRITTERS, INDONESIAN STYLE

SERVES 6 | SERVE HOT OFF THE PAN OR AT ROOM TEMPERATURE
LEFTOVERS KEEP FOR 3 DAYS IN THE FRIDGE | FREEZE FOR 1 MONTH

Corn fritters in a *parev* version – one that can be eaten both with milk and meat dishes – are generally tasteless and not worth the effort. But that can't be said for this delicious recipe, which I have adapted from Sri Owen's wonderful book on Indonesian food and cooking. They also make very interesting finger food for a drinks party.

1 aubergine

salt

1½ tbsp sunflower oil

4 shallots, finely chopped

½ tsp chilli powder

2 garlic cloves, finely chopped

1 tsp ground coriander

½ tsp salt

325g/11 oz canned crisp sweetcorn

1 egg, beaten

4 tbsp plain flour

1 tsp baking powder

2½ tbsp thinly sliced spring onions

100ml/3½ fl oz plus 1 tbsp oil, for shallow frying

Peel the aubergine and cut into 1 cm/³⁄₈in dice, then put in a colander or salad spinner and sprinkle with salt. Leave for 30–40 minutes, then rinse and squeeze as dry as possible.

In a heavy sauté or frying pan, heat 2 tablespoons of oil and stir-fry the shallots, chilli powder and garlic for 2 minutes. Add the aubergine, stir well and season with the coriander and salt. Simmer together for 4 minutes until the aubergine is tender, then set aside to cool.

Put the drained sweetcorn in a bowl. Add the aubergine mixture and all the remaining ingredients, apart from the oil for frying, and mix well. Re-season if necessary. Heat the oil in the sauté pan and drop the mixture by heaped tablespoons into it (it should sizzle), then flatten each fritter lightly with the back of a fork. Cook over a moderate heat for 3 minutes on each side. Serve hot or at room temperature.

You can keep the fritters hot at 110°C/225°F/Gas ½ for up to 30 minutes.

Leftover cold fritters can be gently reheated under the grill.

FLUFFY MASHED POTATOES

SERVES 4–6 | MAKE AND EAT THE SAME DAY

900 g–1.5kg/2–3lb potatoes, peeled and quartered

2 tsp salt

125ml/4 fl oz hot milk

50g/2oz/4 tbsp butter

¼ tsp white pepper or 10 grinds of black pepper

¼ tsp freshly grated nutmeg (optional)

Put the potatoes in a large saucepan and cover with boiling water. Add the salt, bring back to the boil, cover and cook at a steady boil for 15 minutes, or until absolutely tender when pierced with a vegetable knife.

Drain, return to the stove in the same pan and shake over a gentle heat until all the moisture has evaporated. Pour the milk down the side of the pan and when it starts to steam, add the butter, white pepper and nutmeg, if using. Whisk on a very low heat until the potatoes lighten and look fluffy. Add more milk if the mixture seems too dry. Taste and add more salt if necessary. Pile into a warm vegetable dish – and serve immediately.

PERFECT ROAST POTATOES

SERVES 4–6 | SERVE HOT FROM THE OVEN

900g–1.5kg/2–3lb potatoes, peeled and cut into 2.5m/1in slices

salt

oil

margarine

160°C/325°F/Gas 3	1¾ hours
180°C/350°F/Gas 4	1½ hours
190°C/375°F/Gas 5	1½ hours
200°C/400°F/Gas 6	1¼ hours
220°C/425°F/Gas 7	1¼ hours

Put the potatoes in a large saucepan half-full of boiling water, add 1 teaspoon salt and bring slowly back to the boil. Cook until almost but not quite tender – about 15–20 minutes. Drain the potatoes, then return them to the empty saucepan and shake over a low heat until absolutely dry.

Meanwhile, preheat the oven to the temperature on the left that is best for whatever roast is cooking at the same time. Put in the oven a shallow roasting tin just large enough to hold the potato slices in one layer, with a thin layer of oil covering the bottom.

Put the tin of hot oil on the stove, add a knob of margarine, then carefully lay the potatoes in it and immediately turn them over to coat them with the hot fat. Sprinkle lightly with the salt then roast, turning once or twice, for the time given on the left.

CRISPY SAUTÉED POTATOES

SERVES 4 | SERVE HOT OFF THE PAN

900g/2lb potatoes, scrubbed

sea salt

2 tbsp flavourless oil such as sunflower or light olive oil

50g/2oz/4 tbsp butter or margarine

Cook the potatoes, whole in their skins, in boiling salted water for 25–40 minutes, depending on size. Drain and return to the empty saucepan to dry over a low heat, then cool, skin and into thick slices or dice. To fry, put the oil and butter in a very large heavy frying pan. When it starts to foam, add the potatoes and cook very gently for 15 minutes, shaking the pan occasionally so that the potatoes absorb the fat rather than fry in it and turn golden. Increase the heat to make them crisp. Drain from the fat – there should be very little left, put in a dish and sprinkle with salt and pepper and serve at once.

OVEN-CRISP POTATOES

SERVES 6
PARTLY COOKED KEEP FOR 1 DAY IN THE FRIDGE | DO NOT FREEZE

1kg/2¼lb potatoes, scrubbed

1 tsp salt, for boiling

50g/2oz/4 tbsp butter or margarine with 2 tbsp sunflower oil, or 100 ml/3fl oz sunflower or vegetable oil

2 onions, chopped if you are dicing your potatoess, or sliced if you are slicing your potatoes

TO SERVE

a little sea salt

10 grinds of black pepper

1 tbsp chopped parsley

Cook the potatoes, whole in their skins, in boiling salted water for 25–40 minutes until tender. Drain and return to the empty saucepan to dry over a low heat, then cool, skin, if you wish, cut into 1cm/½in slices or dice. Heat the fat in a frying pan and heat until the warmth can be felt on the hand held 5cm/2in above it. Add the onions and potatoes and cook gently for 10 minutes, stirring, until soft and golden. They should slowly absorb the fat rather than fry in it. Transfer to an oven tray wide enough to hold them in one layer – a 35 x 25 x 5cm/14 x 10 x 2in roulade tin is ideal. Leave until 40 minutes before serving. Put the dish in the oven at 220°C/425°F/Gas 7 for 30–40 minutes until crisp and golden, shaking occasionally. The potatoes will take longer to crisp at a lower temperature. The potatoes can be kept hot for up to 20 minutes at 180°C/350°F/Gas 4. Turn into a serving dish, season with sea salt and black pepper and toss with the parsley. Serve piping hot.

BREAD, BAKES AND DESSERTS

RYE AND CARAWAY BREAD

MAKES 3 MEDIUM OR 2 LARGE LOAVES | KEEPS MOIST FOR 4–5 DAYS LOOSELY WRAPPED IN A PLASTIC BAG | FREEZES FOR 3 MONTHS

I am often asked for a recipe for a 'real old-fashioned rye bread'. But which bread, since there are literally dozens that qualify for that description? I chose this one because the method is simpler than most, yet the result is a light, moist, delicious loaf. Including beer gives the bread the traditional, tangy taste without the complexities of using a sour-dough starter.

14g/½oz/4 tsp easy-blend yeast, or 25g/1oz/½ cake fresh yeast

1 tbsp light soft brown sugar

575g/1¼lb strong white bread flour, plus extra for dusting

350g/12oz rye flour

3 tsp salt

3 tsp caraway seeds

425ml/15fl oz beer

150ml/5fl oz warm water

FOR THE GLAZE

1 tsp hot water and 1 tsp brown sugar, or 1 tsp potato flour and 2 tsp cold water

85ml/3fl oz boiling water

Most of the preparation for the bread is done the day before baking, so you may need to plan ahead. Use a mixer rather than a food processor. The recipe makes three loaves which freeze well. Potato flour is available in kosher supermarkets, health food stores and shops specializing in East European ingredients.

With easy-blend yeast, fit the dough hook in the electric mixer, and mix together the yeast, brown sugar, both flours, salt and 2 teaspoons of the caraway seeds. Add the beer mixed with the warm water and mix to a dough.

With fresh yeast, crumble the yeast into a large mixing bowl, add the warm water and brown sugar, stir well and leave for 10 minutes, or until frothy. Add the beer, then, using the K beater of the electric mixer, add the well-mixed flours, salt and 2 teaspoons of the caraway seeds, a cupful at a time until the dough becomes too thick to continue. Change to the dough hook and add the remaining flour, mixing until it forms a dough.

Knead for 3–4 minutes until the dough has a silky, rather limp texture. Turn out on to a lightly floured surface, knead gently into a ball, then put in a well-oiled container large enough to let it expand to 3 times its size. Turn it over to make sure it is lightly coated with oil, cover with a lid or cling film and refrigerate overnight.

Continued on page 138

Next day, leave the dough (still in the container) in the warm kitchen for 1½ hours until it has lost its chill (or warm on defrost in the microwave for 1 minute), then turn it out on to a floured surface and knead gently but firmly to expel all the gas bubbles.

Divide into three 450g/1 lb pieces. Knead each piece into a round or baton and arrange well apart on greased baking trays.

To make the glaze, either mix the hot water and sugar until dissolved, or mix the potato flour and cold water to a smooth, lump-free paste, then gradually whisk the boiling water into either mixture until you have thick, clear paste.

Brush the loaves with your chosen glaze, scatter with the remaining caraway seeds and make 2 slanting slashes in the top with a sharp, floured knife. Slip each tray into a large plastic carrier bag and leave until they have almost doubled in size and feel spongy to the touch – this will take about an 1 hour in a warm kitchen.

Meanwhile, preheat the oven to 200°C/400°F/Gas 6. Bake the loaves for 35–40 minutes, or until they are a deep chestnut colour. If you are using the potato flour to glaze, brush the loaves again 15 minutes before the end of the baking time. Leave on a cooling rack until cold.

BAGELS

MAKES 15 BAGELS | PICTURED ON PAGE 142

Once you know that they must be boiled before they are baked, it is surprisingly easy to produce professional-looking bagels at home. As you can make 15 bagels from just over 375g/13oz flour, it is worthwhile making a stock for the freezer, particularly if you live a long way from a source of good, authentic bagels.

The dough This is identical to the dough used for challah (see page 140), with the exception of the flour. As bagels are much firmer in texture than bread, use a little more flour than in the challah recipe – 375g/13oz of flour, instead of 350g/12oz.

Mix and refrigerate the dough for 9–12 hours or overnight in exactly the same way as for challah. The difference in technique starts once the risen dough is taken from the fridge.

To shape the bagels, work with the chilled dough direct from the fridge. Divide it into 15 pieces. Shape each bagel as follows.

Form the piece into a ball, then flatten with the palm of the hand and roll into a rope 18cm/7in long and 1cm/½in thick.

Wind the rope round the knuckles of your hand. Press on the work surface to seal the joint, then roll it gently back and forth to seal it firmly. Slip the bagel off the knuckles on to a floured board. Repeat with all the pieces of dough.

Leave to rise for an hour until the bagels have increased slightly in size but are not as puffy as rolls. Preheat the oven to maximum (ideally 250°C/500°F/Gas 10) and a very large pan of boiling water ready on the stove.

Put 5 or 6 bagels at a time into the boiling water and boil for 2 minutes, turning them over with a slotted spoon as they rise to the top. Drain from the water and lay on a cooling rack set over a board. Repeat with the remaining bagels. If you wish, dip the boiled bagels into a bowl of poppy or sesame seeds to coat.

Put the bagels on a floured baking sheet and put in the hot oven for 1 minute to dry the top surface, then turn and bake for a further 15 minutes until they are a rich shiny brown.

CHALLAH

This is best made in a mixer rather than a food processor.

150ml/5fl oz warm water

350g/12oz strong white bread flour, plus extra for dusting

14g/¹/₂oz/¼ cake fresh yeast, or 7g/¼oz/2 tsp easy-blend yeast

25g/1oz/2 tbsp sugar or 1 rounded tbsp clear honey (this can be reduced to 1 tbsp if preferred)

¾ tsp salt

2 tbsp sunflower or other flavourless oil

1 large egg

FOR THE GLAZE

1 egg yolk

1 tsp water

1 good pinch of salt

poppy seeds or sesame seeds

If using easy-blend yeast, mix the yeast thoroughly with the other dry ingredients, then add all the remaining ingredients to the bowl.

If using fresh yeast, attach the dough hook to the mixer, then put the water into the mixing bowl, followed by a third of the flour, the crumbled yeast and the sugar or honey. Mix until smooth – about 2 minutes – then cover with a tea towel and leave for 10–15 minutes until it has frothed up. Add all the remaining ingredients for the dough.

Now mix at low speed until a sticky ball begins to form, then turn to medium speed, and knead for 4–5 minutes until the dough is slapping against the edges of the bowl, leaving it clean as it goes round. If it still looks very sticky, work in a further 1–2 tablespoons of flour; if dry, add water a teaspoon at a time until the dough reaches the right consistency.

Tip the dough onto a floured board and knead with the hands for a further minute until it is tight and springy with a silky feel – as smooth as a baby's cheek! Grease a large bowl with oil, turn the dough in it to coat all sides with oil (this stops the surface drying out), cover with cling film and leave to rise in the fridge. If it rises before you have time to deal with it (it takes 9–12 hours but can be left for up to 24 hours), punch it down and leave it to rise again.

To shape the loaves, take the risen dough from the fridge and leave it to come to room temperature in the kitchen – about 1 hour. Or put it in the defrost cycle of the microwave oven for 1 1/2–2 minutes until warm to the touch.

Divide the dough in half and work on each half as follows. Knead the dough by hand or machine to break down any large bubbles of gas, then leave for 5 minutes under a cloth to 'relax'.

To make a 3-strand plait, divide the piece of dough into 3. Flatten each piece with a fist, then roll up into a little Swiss roll. Flatten again, roll up as before, then shape into a ball – this greatly improves the texture of the loaf.

Roll each ball into a 30cm/12in strand that tapers slightly at each end. Join the 3 strands firmly together at one end, then fan them out on the board. Plait in the usual way. Arrange on a greased tray.

To make a tin loaf, lightly grease a 900g/2lb loaf tin measuring about 22.5 x 12.5 x 7.5cm/about 9 x 5 x 3in. Divide the remaining dough into 3 and flatten each piece with the fist, then roll up into a little Swiss roll, flatten, roll up again, then finally roll into a ball. Arrange 2 of the balls side by side in the centre of the tin. Divide the third ball in half, then shape it into two smaller balls and place these on either side of the centre balls. Brush with the glaze and scatter with poppy or sesame seeds.

To prove either the plait or the tin loaf, slip the tray or the loaf tin into a large plastic bag. This creates a miniature 'greenhouse' atmosphere – damp and free from draughts – which the dough needs to rise. Leave in a warm place for 45 minutes to 1 hour, or until puffy again. Remove from the bag.

To bake the bread, preheat the oven to 230°C/450°F/Gas 8. Put the bread in the oven and immediately turn the temperature down to 200°C/400°F/Gas 6. Bake the plait for 25–30 minutes or until crusty and brown; bake the loaf for 30–40 minutes, or until the bottom sounds hollow when tapped.

GERMAN BUTTER KUCHEN WITH DATE FILLING

**MAKES 1 LARGE LOAF | KEEPS FOR FRESH 2 DAYS IN THE FRIDGE.
COOKED KUCHEN FREEZES FOR 3 MONTHS; UNRISEN DOUGH FOR 3 MONTHS;
SHAPED BUT UNCOOKED KUCHEN FOR 2 WEEKS**

This butter cake is delicious when sliced and spread with butter, low-fat spread or cream cheese. It is also good to eat if toasted when it begins to dry out after a few days.

1 quantity risen kuchen dough (see page 182)

a little flour, for dusting

FOR THE DATE FILLING

225g/8oz pitted dried dates, chopped

15g/½oz/1 tbsp butter or margarine

1½ tsp ground cinnamon

4 tbsp sultanas

FOR THE ICING

50g/2oz sifted icing sugar

2 tsp lemon or orange juice

25g /1oz chopped walnuts

FOR THE CINNAMON RAISIN FILLING

2 tbsp butter

50g/2oz light soft brown sugar

1 tsp ground cinnamon

50g/2oz sultanas

To make the filling, put all the ingredients into a pan, cover and simmer, stirring occasionally, until the mixture forms a thick, juicy paste. Allow to cool.

Grease a 900g/2lb loaf tin measuring about 23 x 13 x 7.5cm/9 x 5 x 3in. Roll out the dough on a lightly floured board into a rectangle 2.5cm/1in wider than the base of the loaf tin and 1cm/½in thick. Spread with the filling to within 1cm/½in of either side, then turn these sides over the filling to seal it in, and roll up tightly into a Swiss roll. Lay it in the tin, join-side down. Put the tin into a large plastic bag and leave in a warm place until the kuchen looks puffy and feels spongy to the touch – 30–40 minutes.

Meanwhile, preheat the oven to 180°C/350°F/Gas 4. Bake the kuchen for 35–40 minutes until golden brown and firm to a gentle touch. Turn on to a cooling rack and, while still warm, spread with the icing made by adding just enough fruit juice to the icing sugar to make a thick, coating consistency. Decorate with the nuts.

VARIATION
CINNAMON RAISIN FILLING
Mix all the ingredients (left) together until spreadable. Use to fill the kuchen as before.

FRUITED KUCHEN RING

MAKES A 23CM/9IN CAKE

½ quantity risen kuchen dough
(see page 182)

FOR THE FILLING

50g/2oz sugar

1 tsp cinnamon

2 tbsp melted butter

50g/2oz raisins

FOR THE GLAZE

1 tbsp lemon juice

75g/3oz icing sugar

Roll the dough into a rectangle about 28cm/11 ¼in by 15cm/6in. Combine the filling ingredients then spread in an even layer over the dough. Starting at the long side nearest to you, roll up into a tight roll, then join the ends together to form a ring. Line a baking tray with parchment paper and transfer the ring to it. Using kitchen scissors, make cuts two-thirds of the way through the dough at 4cm/1 ½in to reveal some of the filling. Slip the tray into a large plastic bag and leave to rise in a warm place until puffy, this should take about 30 minutes. Preheat the oven to 200°C/400°F/Gas 6. Bake the ring for 25 minutes. Beat the glaze ingredients together until smooth then drizzle over the warm kuchen.

SCHNECKEN
GERMAN SWEET BUNS

MAKES 12

KEEPS FOR 2 DAYS IN THE FRIDGE | FREEZES FOR 3 MONTHS

½ quantity risen kuchen dough
(see page 182)

FOR THE GLAZE

2 tbsp butter

2 tbsp brown sugar

2 tbsp golden syrup

FOR THE FILLING

2 tbsp soft butter

50g/2oz caster sugar

1 tsp ground cinnamon

50g/2oz raisins

25g/1oz chopped walnuts

Simmer the glaze ingredients in a pan for 1 minute, or until a rich golden brown. Divide between 12 greased bun tins.

For the filling, put the butter in a bowl and beat in the sugar and cinnamon, then the raisins and walnuts. Roll out the dough on a lightly floured board to 1cm/½in thick, in a rectangle 30 x 15cm/12 x 6in. Spread with the filling. Roll up lengthways into a tight roll, then cut into 2.5cm/1in slices. Arrange these, cut-side up, in the bun tins. Slip the tray into a plastic carrier bag and leave until puffy – 30–40 minutes. Meanwhile, preheat the oven to 200°C/400°F/Gas 6. Bake the buns for 15–20 minutes, or until a rich brown. Allow 5 minutes for the glaze to set a little, then remove the schnecken from the tins and leave them, with the glaze on top, on a cooling rack.

TRADITIONAL CHEESECAKE

SERVES 10

KEEPS FOR 3 DAYS IN THE FRIDGE | FREEZES FOR 2 MONTHS

This is an updated version of the traditional cheesecake from Eastern Europe that used to be made with home-made kaese (curd cheese) and baked in a pastry case. It is rather more luxurious than older recipes, but as most of us make this cake only on special occasions, I think it is worth putting in the finest ingredients and making it in a size to serve a crowd.

1 recipe quantity cheesecake pastry crust (see page 183)

FOR THE FILLING

3 eggs, separated

1 pinch of salt

350g/12oz low- or medium-fat soft cheese

50g/2oz ground almonds

25g/1oz/2 tbsp soft butter

50g/2oz caster sugar

3 tbsp lemon juice

grated zest of ½ lemon

½ tsp vanilla extract

5 heaped tbsp sultanas

FOR DECORATION

1 tbsp granulated sugar

25g/1oz flaked almonds

Preheat the oven to 180°C/350°F/Gas 4.

Put the egg yolks and whites in separate bowls. Add the salt to the egg whites and whisk until they hold floppy peaks. Add all the remaining ingredients except the sultanas to the egg yolks and mix until thoroughly blended. Carefully fold the egg whites into the cheese mixture. Stir in the sultanas, then pour into the unbaked pastry case.

Take the egg white left over from making the pastry and whisk until frothy. Paint it over the cheese mixture, then sprinkle with the granulated sugar. Scatter with the almonds.

Bake the larger flan for 40 minutes, the smaller, deeper flan for 20 minutes, then turn the oven down to 160°C/325°F/Gas 3 and bake for a further 30 minutes. In either case, the cheesecake is ready when it is a pale gold colour and firm to gentle touch round the edges. (The filling continues to set as it cools.) Loosen the edges with a knife as soon as possible to help prevent cracking.

LUSCIOUS LEMON CAKE

MAKES A 15CM/6IN SQUARE CAKE
KEEPS FOR 1 WEEK IN THE FRIDGE IN AN AIRTIGHT CONTAINER
FREEZES FOR 3 MONTHS

This delicate sponge, moistened with a tart lemon syrup, must be the all-time family favourite, and is the star of a thousand cake stalls. The cake will stay moist for as long as as any of it remains uneaten!

125g/4oz soft butter or margarine

175g/6oz caster sugar

175g/6oz self-raising flour

5 generous tbsp milk

grated zest of 1 lemon

2 large eggs

pinch of salt

FOR THE LEMON SYRUP

75g/3oz icing sugar, plus extra for dusting

Juice of 1 ½ large lemons

Preheat the oven to 180°C/350°F/Gas 4. Oil a 15cm/6in square cake tin and line the bottom with parchment paper – this is important. (Alternatively, oil and line a 900g/2lb loaf tin, 22.5 x 12.5 x 7.5cm/ 9 x 5 x 3in).

Put all the cake ingredients into a bowl and beat by mixer or wooden spoon until smooth – about 3 minutes. Pour the cake mixture into the tin and smooth the top with the back of a spoon. Bake for 45 minutes.

Remove from the oven and stand the cake, still in the tin, on a cooling rack. Gently heat the sugar and lemon juice just until a clear syrup is formed. Prick the warm cake all over with a fork, then gently pour the syrup over it, spooning it from the sides until it has been completely absorbed.

Leave until the cake is cold, then carefully turn out. Serve dusted with icing sugar.

LITHUANIAN CHOCOLATE AND NUT TORTE

MAKES A 20CM/8IN CAKE
KEEPS FOR 1 WEEK IN AN AIRTIGHT CONTAINER IN THE FRIDGE | FREEZES FOR 3 MONTHS

This kind of flourless chocolate cake is made all over the Baltic States and the countries of the former Austro-Hungarian Empire. It is moist yet light in texture, worthy of a special occasion.

100g/4oz ground almonds

3 tbsp fine dry breadcrumbs

100g/4oz good-quality dark eating chocolate, grated

3 large eggs, separated

125g/4½oz caster sugar

1 tbsp lemon juice

FOR THE COATING

1 tbsp strong coffee or 2 tsp instant coffee dissolved in 1 tbsp hot water

1 tbsp Tia Maria or similar coffee liqueur

3 tbsp drinking chocolate

75g/3oz/6 tbsp butter, softened

75g/3oz icing sugar

TO SERVE

8 whole blanched almonds, toasted in a dry pan

Preheat the oven to 180°C/350°F/Gas 4. Have ready a 20cm/8in round loose-bottomed tin, greased and lined with baking parchment.

Mix the ground almonds, crumbs and the grated chocolate. Whisk the egg whites until they hold stiff peaks, then add the sugar a tablespoon at a time, whisking until stiff after each addition. Fold in the egg yolks, followed by the dry ingredients. Finally, stir in the lemon juice. Spoon the mixture into the prepared tin and level the top.

Bake for 45 minutes until golden brown and firm to a gentle touch – a skewer inserted in the centre should come out clean. Leave on a cooling rack until cold, then carefully turn out.

To make the icing, put the coffee, liqueur and chocolate in a bowl and mix well. Stir in the butter and icing sugar and beat until smooth. Coat the cake with the icing and decorate with toasted almonds.

APPLE STREUSEL KUCHEN

MAKES A 12 X 9CM/4½ X 3½IN KUCHEN
MAKE AND EAT THE SAME DAY

This is delicious served hot or cold. A layer of thinly sliced apple is sandwiched between the kuchen batter. It is best the same day, before the topping goes soft.

1 quantity quick kuchen batter (see page 183)

600g/1lb 5oz cooking apples (weight before peeling)

FOR THE TOPPING

50g/2oz flour

2 tsp ground cinnamon

150g/5oz light brown sugar

4 tbsp butter

Preheat the oven to 190°C/375°F/Gas 5.

Mix together the flour, cinnamon and sugar. Melt the butter, then pour on to the dry ingredients and blend with a fork until evenly moistened.

Evenly spread the kuchen dough in a greased baking tin measuring 30 x 23 x 4cm/12 x 9 x ½in. Peel, core and quarter the apples, then cut into thin slices 3mm/⅛in thick. Arrange the apple slices in overlapping rows so that the kuchen batter is completely covered.

Sprinkle the topping over the unbaked kuchen and bake for 30–40 minutes, or until the cake has shrunk from the sides of the tin, the apples feel tender when pierced with a knife and the streusel is golden brown.

Alternatively, to make an apple kuchen (as pictured), prepare the ingredients as above, without sprinkling the crumble mixture over the top, and bake as before until golden brown.

DUTCH APPLE SPONGE

MAKES 12 GOOD-SIZED SQUARES
KEEPS FOR 2 DAYS IN THE FRIDGE | FREEZES FOR 3 MONTHS

On a cold winter's night, how good it is to come home to a nice, comforting hot pud! And it doesn't have to be unhealthy, either. With lots of fruit, unrefined sugar and a sponge made with wholemeal flour, it can be nutritious as well as warming and delicious. Although best served hot, if there is any left over, this doubles as a very respectable apple cake.

250g/9oz wholemeal self-raising flour, or 250g/9oz white or wholemeal plain flour plus 2 tsp baking powder

1 tsp baking powder

125g/4oz light brown sugar

3 eggs

125ml/4fl oz water

75g/3oz/6 tbsp soft margarine

1 tsp grated lemon zest

FOR THE TOPPING

900g/2lb large tart eating apples such as Cox's or Braeburn

2½ tbsp lemon juice

50g/2oz/4 tbsp margarine, melted

125g/4oz soft brown sugar

1½ tsp ground cinnamon

Preheat the oven to 200°C/400°F/Gas 6. Grease a shallow cake tin about 30 x 20cm/12 x 8in. Place all the cake ingredients in a bowl and mix until smooth – 3 minutes by hand, 2 minutes by electric mixer, 20 seconds by food processor, scraping down the sides halfway with a rubber spatula. Spoon into the tin and smooth the top level with a knife.

Peel, core and slice the apples 3mm/⅛in thick. Toss the apples in a bowl with the lemon juice, then arrange in tightly packed, overlapping rows on top of the cake mixture, covering it completely. Drizzle the melted margarine on top, and sprinkle evenly with the sugar and cinnamon mixed together.

Bake for around 45 minutes until the cake is a rich brown and the apples are tender. Serve warm or at room temperature with cream, ice cream, or Greek yogurt drizzled with honey.

APPLE CRISP

SERVES 6
KEEPS FOR 3 DAYS IN THE FRIDGE | FREEZES FOR 3 MONTHS

This recipe is simple to make, uncomplicated in flavour and utterly delicious to eat. It works equally well with pitted plums, or a combination of plums and apples.

4 large cooking apples (or a mixture of Macintosh and Granny Smiths)

50g/2oz brown sugar mixed with ½ tsp ground cinnamon

1 tbsp lemon juice

75ml/3fl oz/6 tbsp water

FOR THE TOPPING

75g/3oz flour

25g/1oz/3 tbsp porridge (rolled) oats

125g/4oz soft brown sugar

75g/3oz/6 tbsp) margarine or butter

custard or yogurt, to serve (opltional)

Preheat the oven to 190°C/375°F/Gas 5. Peel, core and slice the apples into a shallow baking or gratin dish approximately 27.5 x 20 x 4cm/11 x 8 x 1½in deep. Sprinkle them with the mixed sugar and cinnamon followed by the lemon juice and water.

For the topping, combine the flour, oats and brown sugar, then gently rub in the fat until the mixture is crumbly. Sprinkle in an even layer over the apples.

Bake for 1 hour, or until crunchy and golden brown. Serve plain or with custard or yogurt.

FAYE'S NEW-STYLE LOKSHEN PUDDING

SERVES 6

LEFTOVERS KEEP FOR 3 DAYS IN THE FRIDGE | FREEZE FOR 3 MONTHS

This is a fruitier version of the traditional noodle pudding, sweetened by a little honey instead of a lot of sugar. It does not have the crustiness of the original but is altogether lighter in texture.

225g/8oz dried broad egg noodles

2 eating apples

125g/4oz glacé cherries

50g/2oz margarine

125g/4oz sultanas

125g/4oz raisins

1 egg

1 tsp ground allspice

2½ tbsp orange juice

1 rounded tbsp mild honey

Break the noodles into small pieces and boil until tender. Peel, core and grate the apples, wash and slice the cherries, melt the margarine.

Mix all the ingredients gently but firmly together, then turn into a greased 1.2l/2 pint pudding basin or heatproof bowl. Cover with foil and bake at 150°C/300°F/Gas 2 for 1½ hours. Turn out and serve plain or with fresh strawberries.

MIRKATAN
ARMENIAN FRUIT COMPÔTE

SERVES 6 | PICTURED ON PAGE 9
KEEPS FOR 4 DAYS IN THE FRIDGE | DO NOT FREEZE

In this ancient Armenian recipe, plump and juicy dried fruits mixed with nuts and sections of orange are macerated in a delicately spiced wine syrup. The compôte can be served either warm or cold, plain or accompanied in the traditional manner by rosewater-scented whipped cream or, as I prefer it, with Greek yogurt lightly sweetened with Hymettus honey.

175g/6oz pitted prunes

175g/6oz dried apricots

175g/6oz dried peaches or pears

freshly brewed tea to cover the dried fruit

50g/2oz walnut halves

water

100ml/3fl oz fruity red wine

3 strips of orange zest

1 cinnamon stick

50g/2oz caster sugar

1 tbsp fresh lemon juice

1 tbsp orange blossom water

2 navel oranges, peeled and sectioned

The day before, put the dried fruit in a bowl and pour the strained tea over it. Cover and leave overnight.

Next day, strain into a bowl (reserving the liquid) and insert the walnut halves into the prunes. Make up the reserved tea with water, if necessary, to 200ml/7fl oz. Put in a wide pan together with the wine, orange rind, cinnamon stick and sugar. Bring to the boil and simmer, uncovered, for 3 minutes.

Add the dried fruit, cover and simmer for 20 minutes until the fruit is tender and the syrup has thickened. Stir in the lemon juice, orange blossom water and orange sections. Serve hot or cold.

TRADITIONAL KICHELS

MAKES ABOUT 50, DEPENDING ON SIZE
KEEP FOR 2 WEEKS IN AN AIRTIGHT CONTAINER | FREEZE FOR 3 MONTHS

These orange and vanilla biscuits are a favourite for all kinds of occasions because they do not include any dairy products and so are suitable to serve before, with or after either a meat or a dairy meal. Use only the minimum amount of flour needed to achieve a rollable dough, and the kichels will be light and crisp.

2 large eggs

150g/5oz caster sugar, plus extra for sprinkling

125ml/4fl oz sunflower or other flavourless oil

grated zest of 1 orange

1 tsp vanilla extract

300–350g/11–12oz plain flour mixed with 3 tsp baking powder

Preheat the oven to 180°C/350°F/Gas 4 and line 2 baking sheets with baking parchment.

Whisk the eggs until thick, then gradually whisk in the sugar, followed by the oil, the orange zest and the vanilla. Finally stir in enough flour to make a rollable, non-sticky dough. Knead until smooth, then roll out 1cm/½in thick on a floured board.

Sprinkle the dough with caster sugar, then roll lightly to press in the sugar. Cut into shapes with biscuit cutters and arrange on the prepared trays, leaving room for the biscuits to spread. Bake for 20–25 minutes, or until a pale gold in colour. Leave on wire racks until cold.

JUDEBROD
DANISH CARDAMOM BISCUITS

MAKES ABOUT 60
KEEP FOR 1 WEEK IN AN AIRTIGHT CONTAINER | FREEZE FOR 6 WEEKS

Cardamom – that wonderfully aromatic spice which gives authentic Danish pastries their unique flavour – magically transforms these quickly made, melt-in-the-mouth biscuits into very special petits fours to serve with a compôte of summer fruits or ice cream.

120g/4¼oz butter, cut into roughly 2.5cm/1in chunks

125g/4oz light muscovado sugar

1 tsp ground cinnamon

1 tsp freshly pounded or ready-ground cardamom seeds

1 egg

1 tsp baking powder

250g/9oz plain flour

FOR THE DECORATION

25g/1oz/2 tbsp brown or white coarse sugar

25g/1oz flaked almonds

By hand or electric mixer, work all the ingredients together until a dough is formed.

By food processor, put all the ingredients in the food processor bowl and process or pulse just until little moist balls of dough are beginning to form. Tip out into a bowl and knead into a dough.

Flatten into a block 2.5cm/1in thick, then chill for several hours or overnight.

Preheat the oven to 190°C/375°F/Gas 5 and grease or line baking sheets with baking parchment. Mix the coarse sugar and flaked almonds together.

Roll out the dough 3mm/⅛in thick and stamp out 5cm/2in rounds with a cutter. Brush them lightly with water, then dip them into the sugar and almond mixture (or sprinkle this mixture on top).

Place the biscuits on the prepared baking sheets and bake for 10–12 minutes, or until firm to the touch. Leave on wire racks until cold.

GEREYBES
SEPHARDI SHORTBREAD 'BRACELETS'

MAKES ABOUT 36
KEEP FOR 2 WEEKS IN AN AIRTIGHT CONTAINER AT ROOM TEMPERATURE
| FREEZE FOR 3 MONTHS

The baking of the Sephardim, particularly those from communities in the Middle East, is of a delicacy and refinement rarely equalled in Western cooking. Craft plays a great part in shaping the many different kinds of pastries of which this delicate butter biscuit is typical. This recipe comes from a family with roots in the Damascus of the late 19th century.

225g/8oz unsalted butter, at room temperature

150g/5oz caster sugar

350g/12oz plain flour, plus extra for dusting

50g/2oz split blanched almonds

Preheat the oven to 160°C/325°F/Gas 3.

Using an electric mixer, cream the butter until it is like mayonnaise, then gradually add the sugar, beating until the mixture is almost white. Add the flour a little at a time, beating after each addition. When enough flour has been added, the dough will come away from the edges of the bowl.

Turn out on to a lightly floured board and knead gently but thoroughly until the dough is quite smooth. Take a piece of the dough and roll into a salami shape about 2.5cm/1in in diameter, then cut across at 1cm/½in intervals into short pieces. Roll each of these in turn into a pencil shape about 13cm/5in long. Form into a 'bracelet' by slightly overlapping the ends, then put a split almond over the join. Repeat with the remaining dough.

Arrange on ungreased baking trays leaving 2.5cm/1in between each biscuit. Bake for 18–20 minutes, or until the biscuits are barely coloured and just firm to the touch – do not overbrown or the delicate flavour will be compromised. Leave on the trays until cold. Store in an airtight container.

APPLE BUWELE
PASTRY-WRAPPED APPLE

SERVES 6
KEEPS FOR 3 DAYS IN THE FRIDGE | FREEZE UNTIL REQUIRED

Wrapped in tender yeast dough, a cinnamon-scented apple filling is the heart of a famous South German Jewish dish traditionally served at Sukkot.

FOR THE YEAST PASTRY

450g/1lb plain flour, plus extra for dusting

½ tsp salt

7g/¼oz/2 tsp easy-blend yeast, or 14g/½oz/½ cake fresh yeast

75g/3oz caster sugar

2 eggs

150ml/5fl oz milk or water

75g/3oz soft butter or margarine, or 125ml/4fl oz oil

FOR THE APPLE FILLING

675g/1½lb Bramley cooking apples

25g/1oz/2 tbsp butter or margarine

75g/3oz light brown soft sugar

1 tbsp lemon juice

3 tbsp raisins or sultanas

FOR THE ICING

75g/3oz icing sugar

1 tbsp lemon juice

a few flaked almonds

To make the pastry, mix the flour, salt, yeast and sugar in a bowl. Put the eggs in a measuring jug and make up to 250ml/9fl oz with hand-hot milk or water, whisking well to blend. Add to the dry ingredients with the soft fat or oil, and mix with a beater or dough hook for about 5 minutes until it forms a soft, shiny ball that leaves the sides of the bowl clean. If it is too soft to gather into a ball, add a little more flour. Turn on to a floured board, knead for 30 seconds, then put into an oiled bowl and turn it over to coat it well with the oil. Cover with cling film. It can now be given 3–4 bursts of 50 per cent power (500W) for 20 seconds each, at 5-minute intervals, in the microwave. This will almost halve the rising time. Otherwise, leave it in a warm place until double in bulk – about 1½ hours. Knead it for 1–2 minutes, then leave for a further 10 minutes.

While the dough is rising the first time, prepare the filling by peeling, coring and thinly slicing the apples, then putting them into a sauté pan with all the remaining ingredients and cooking gently until soft but not mushy. Allow to go quite cold. To shape the strudel, roll the dough into a large rectangle about 1cm/½in thick, spread with the filling, turn in the sides and roll up gently starting from a long edge. Lay on a greased baking tin and bend in a horseshoe shape. Put into a large plastic carrier bag and leave until puffy – about 30 minutes. Preheat the oven to 200°C/400°F/Gas 6. Remove the tray from the bag and bake for 35–40 minutes until a rich brown. Cool for 5 minutes, then brush with the icing made by mixing the sugar and juice until smooth. Sprinkle with the almonds, then leave to cool and set.

VANILLA KIPFERL

MAKES 18
KEEP FOR 2 WEEKS AT ROOM TEMPERATURE IN AN AIRTIGHT CONTAINER FREEZE FOR 3 MONTHS

The pride and joy of every Jewish cook of Austro-Hungarian origin, the kipferl is one of the great biscuits of the world. It has been served in the *konditorei* (coffee houses) of Vienna and Budapest since the 17th century. The biscuits can be made on the board, like shortbread, or in a processor or mixer, but in the latter case take care not to overmix the sugar and butter.

140g/5oz plain flour

1 pinch of salt

25g/1oz ground almonds or hazelnuts, or
a mixture of each

100g/4oz butter at room temperature, cut into 2.5cm/1in chunks

2 tbsp caster sugar

1 tbsp vanilla sugar

1 egg yolk

FOR COATING THE BISCUITS

sifted icing sugar

To make by the traditional method, put the flour, salt and nuts on the board, make a well in the centre and add the butter and sugar. Work these together with the fingers, blend in the egg yolk, then gradually work in the surrounding dry ingredients until a dough is formed.

In the mixer, work the butter, sugar and vanilla sugar together until absorbed. Work in the egg yolk. Gradually add the flour, ground nuts and salt until the dough leaves the side of the bowl clean.

Chill for 1 hour. Preheat the oven to 160°C/325°F/Gas 3. In shaping the biscuits, do not use any flour on the work surface because this will toughen the biscuits. A marble or granite surface is ideal. Pinch off pieces of dough the size of a walnut and roll between the palms into 36 smooth, even balls. Roll each ball under your hand into a 'pencil' about 1cm/½in thick and 9–10cm/3½–4in long, then bend into a crescent. Arrange on ungreased baking sheets, leaving about 2.5cm/1in between each biscuit, as they do spread a little. Bake for 18 minutes, or until a very pale-gold colour (they must not brown). Carefully lift on to a cooling rack with a flat spatula and leave for 3 minutes to firm up, then dip into a bowl of icing sugar. Dip again when completely cold. Allow to mature for 24 hours in an airtight container.

ALMOND MACAROONS

MAKES ABOUT 12
KEEP FOR 1 WEEK IN AN AIRTIGHT CONTAINER IN THE FRIDGE
FREEZE FOR 3 MONTHS

The secret to a good macaroon seems to lie in the amount of egg white used – just the right uncooked texture and the macaroons will bake crisp on the outside and be moist and chewy within.

125g/4oz ground almonds

1½–2 egg whites (40–50ml/
1½–2fl oz) broken up with a fork

150g/5oz caster sugar

20g/¾oz/2 tbsp vanilla sugar

sifted icing sugar

12–13 halves of blanched almonds

Preheat the oven to 200°C/400°F/Gas 6. Cover a baking tray with baking parchment.

Put the ground almonds into the food processor or minichop and process for 15 seconds, or until very finely ground.

Add about half an egg white, and process for another 10 seconds. Then add half the caster sugar and the vanilla sugar, and process for another 10 seconds. Add another half an egg white and the remaining sugar in the same way. Then add a further half egg white. The mixture will now be soft but just capable of being formed into balls with the hands. If it is too stiff, add the remaining half egg white.

Take up pieces of the dough and roll between the hands into balls the size of a large walnut – you should get 12 or 13 balls. If you make more, they're too small and should be re-rolled.

Put the balls 5cm/2in apart on the baking parchment and gently flatten with the fingers. Brush all over with cold water, then sprinkle with the icing sugar. Place an almond half on each one, or leave plain, as you prefer.

Bake for 15–17 minutes, or until the tops are just lightly browned. Over-baking will result in crisp instead of moist macaroons. Remove from the tray using a spatula. When cold, store in an airtight container.

CINNAMON BALLS

MAKES 20–22
KEEP FOR I WEEK IN AN AIRTIGHT CONTAINER AT ROOM TEMPERATURE
FREEZE FOR 3 MONTHS

This must be the definitive recipe for this famous Anglo-Jewish biscuit – a crisp shell enclosing a soft, fudgy interior. The inside will stay soft and moist, provided the cinnamon balls are not over-baked. Delicious with tea or coffee, or as after-dinner petits fours.

2 egg whites

125g/4oz caster sugar

225g/8oz ground almonds

I tbsp ground cinnamon

a small bowl of icing sugar, for coating

Preheat the oven to 160°C/325°F/Gas 3 and grease a baking sheet.

Beat the whites until they form stiff peaks. Stir in all the remaining ingredients, mixing until even in colour. Form into 20–22 balls with wetted hands and arrange on the prepared baking sheet.

Bake for 18–20 minutes, or until just firm to the touch. Roll in icing sugar while warm and then again when cold.

VARIATION
CINNAMON AND WALNUT BALLS
Fold in 2oz/50g finely chopped walnuts before forming the balls.

BASICS

RICE AND GRAIN DISHES
COUSCOUS

SERVES 4
KEEPS FOR 2 DAYS IN THE FRIDGE | FREEZES FOR 3 MONTHS

Although fine-grain couscous looks similar to bulgur, couscous is actually a type of dried pasta. The 'grains' are made by rolling moist semolina wheat, then coating them with fine flour. It is traditionally steamed, rather than boiled, to produce a wonderfully light, fluffy texture.

350g/12oz couscous

4 tbsp sunflower or olive oil

1 tsp salt

lukewarm water

Put the couscous and oil in a bowl and add the salt. Add lukewarm water to twice the depth of the couscous, stir well for 1 minute, then drain in a sieve.

For a small quantity, leave in the sieve and steam, covered, over boiling water for 10 minutes until fluffy and separate.

For a larger quantity, line the top of a steamer with a light-coloured non-woven kitchen cloth, add the drained couscous, cover and steam for 10 minutes. Alternatively, in the microwave, reheat, covered, on 100 per cent (1000W) power for 1 – 1½ minutes.

SIMPLE RICE PILAFF

SERVES 6
KEEPS FOR 3 DAYS IN THE FRIDGE | FREEZES FOR 3 MONTHS

Sautéing the rice and onion transforms plain rice into a delicious, savoury side dish.

350g/12oz Basmati rice

3 tbsp oil

1 onion, finely chopped

700ml/1¼ pints hot chicken stock (see page 176)

2 tsp salt

15 grinds of black pepper

Rinse the rice in a sieve under cold water until the water runs clear. Heat the oil in a heavy-based saucepan and cook the onion for 5 minutes until soft and golden. Add the rice and turn in the onion and fat for 3 minutes. Stir in the hot stock, salt and pepper. Bring to the boil, then cover tightly and cook for 20 minutes over a low heat, either on top of the stove, or in the oven at 200°C/400°F/Gas 6. Fluff up the rice with a fork before serving.

TURKISH RICE PILAFF

SERVES 6
KEEPS FOR 3 DAYS IN THE FRIDGE | FREEZES FOR 6 MONTHS

A superbly flavoured dish to serve with roast chicken or lamb chops.

275g/10oz Basmati rice

1 heaped tbsp margarine

1 onion, finely chopped

575ml/1 pint hot chicken stock

¼ tsp turmeric

½ tsp salt

¼ tsp ground cinnamon

50g/2oz sultanas

50g/2oz unsalted pistachios, blanched and halved, or 50g/2oz cashew nuts, toasted in a dry pan

Make in exactly the same way as the plain rice pilaff (above), adding all the seasoning and the sultanas with the hot liquid. Stir in the nuts with a fork just before serving.

PERSIAN CHILAU RICE

SERVES 4 | PICTURED RIGHT
KEEPS FOR 2 DAYS IN THE FRIDGE | FREEZES FOR 3 MONTHS

175g/6oz Basmati rice

1 tbsp salt

1 ½ tbsp sunflower oil

1 tbsp water

3 cardamom pods

Soak the rice in cold water to cover for 30 minutes. Strain and rinse under the cold tap until the water runs clear. Bring a large heavy saucepan of water to the boil with the salt. Add the rice and cook, uncovered, bubbling steadily, for 7 minutes, or until a grain feels almost tender when bitten. Turn into a strainer, rinse thoroughly under the hot tap, then drain well. Put half the oil and the water into the pan and heat until it steams, then add half the rice, the cardamom pods and the remaining oil. Add the rest of the rice. Wrap a tea towel under the lid of the pan, then place it firmly into position so that you have a perfect seal. Leave on the lowest heat for 20 minutes. The result is perfect, fluffy rice. And the crunchy layer that forms on the base of the pan is particularly prized.

PERSIAN CHELLO RICE

SERVES 6.
KEEPS FOR 3 DAYS IN THE FRIDGE | FREEZES FOR 3 MONTHS

300g/11 oz Basmati rice

2 tbsp salt

2 tbsp any oil plus 2 tbsp extra

1 tbsp water

Soak the rice in cold water for 30 minutes, then strain and rinse under running water until the water runs clear. Bring a large heavy saucepan of water to the boil. Add the salt and rice and cook, uncovered, bubbling steadily, for 7 minutes, or until a grain feels almost tender but still has a little bite. Turn the rice into the sieve and rinse under the hot tap, then drain well to remove excess salt. Put the 2 tablespoons oil into the pan with the water and heat until it steams, then spoon in the rice and cover with the second 2 tablespoons of oil. Wrap a tea towel under the lid of the pan, then place it firmly into position so that you have a perfect seal. Steam the rice over a very low heat for 20 minutes. Spoon the rice on to a warm plate, then loosen the crisp layer sticking to the bottom of the pan and stir that into the rice.

SESAME SPICED RICE

SERVES 4

KEEPS FOR 3 DAYS IN THE FRIDGE | FREEZES FOR 3 MONTHS

The addition of a little minced meat simmered in wine gives this rich casserole extra body and flavour. It is a perfect dish to serve at a buffet supper party with cold meat or poultry.

50g/2oz sesame seeds

1 tbsp sunflower oil

1 small onion, finely chopped

225g/8oz minced beef

200g/7oz Basmati or other long-grain rice

150ml/5fl oz full-bodied red wine

1 tbsp dark soy sauce

1 tsp paprika

1 tsp salt

350ml/12fl oz beef or chicken stock

Preheat the oven to 180°C/350°F/Gas 4. Put the sesame seeds on a baking tray and toast in the oven for 10–15 minutes, or until golden brown. Remove.

Meanwhile, gently heat the oil in a flameproof casserole and sauté the onion until soft and golden. Add the meat and cook until it loses its redness and begins to brown, stirring with a fork. Now add the rice and cook until it loses its glassy appearance, stirring well. Pour in the wine and bubble fiercely until its volume is reduced by half. Add the seasonings and stock and bring to a full boil. Stir well and transfer to the oven.

Cook, covered, for 30 minutes until the rice is tender and has absorbed all the liquid. Stir in the toasted sesame seeds.

To reheat from cold, sprinkle the surface lightly with water, cover, then put in a moderate oven at 180°C/350°F/Gas 4 for 15 minutes, or until warm. In the microwave, cook covered on 100 per cent power for 2–3 minutes.

Once cooked, dish can be kept hot in the oven at 150°C/300°F/Gas 2 for up to half an hour.

BULGUR PILAFF

SERVES 4
KEEPS FOR 2 DAYS IN THE FRIDGE | FREEZES FOR 3 MONTHS

This can be served hot as a light and savoury accompaniment or at room temperature with a cold buffet. It is equally tasty either way.

1 small onion, finely chopped

2 tbsp oil

175g/6oz bulgur

1 tsp finely grated orange zest

50g/2oz raisins

425ml/14fl oz chicken stock

salt and ground black pepper

25g/1oz pine nuts, toasted in a dry pan

25g/1oz/2 tbsp chopped parsley (enough to 'green' the pilaff)

4 spring onions, finely sliced

In an 20–23cm/8–9in heavy-based saucepan or sauté pan, fry the onion in the oil over a moderate heat, stirring until softened. Stir in the bulgur and the orange zest and cook the mixture, stirring, for 1 minute. Add the raisins, the stock and salt and pepper to taste, bring the liquid to the boil and cook, covered, over a low heat for 10 minutes, or until the liquid is absorbed.

To serve hot, fluff the pilaff with a fork and stir in the pine nuts, parsley and spring onions. To serve cold, allow the pilaff to cool for 15 minutes before stirring in the remaining ingredients.

This dish reheats well in the microwave – allow 2 minutes in a covered dish on 100 per cent (1000W) power or until piping hot.

TRADITIONAL KASHA

SERVES 6
KEEPS FOR 3 DAYS IN THE FRIDGE | FREEZES FOR 3 MONTHS

Kasha, or roasted buckwheat, has a delicious nutty flavour. You can buy it in whole food shops or online.

225g/8oz kasha (roasted buckwheat)

1 beaten egg

425ml/15fl oz boiling water

2 tsp paprika

1 tsp salt

10 grinds of black pepper

1 large onion, finely chopped

3 tbsp chicken fat or margarine

4–5½ tbsp leftover beef or chicken gravy, optional but very good

Put the uncooked kasha into a large sauté pan and add the beaten egg. Mix well and cook over a medium heat for 5 minutes, stirring occasionally, until the groats look puffy and dry. Add the boiling water and the seasonings, cover and simmer for 15 minutes until the liquid is absorbed.

Meanwhile, gently sauté the onion in the fat in a covered pan until soft and golden, then add to the cooked kasha, stirring well. Stir in the gravy, if using, and reheat until steaming. May be reheated.

VARIATION
Kasha Varnishkes
Add 225g/8oz freshly cooked farfalle to the kasha just before serving and mix well.

MEAT STOCKS

Stock is quite simply a flavoured liquid from which soups and sauces are made. The more flavourful the stock, the tastier the soup or sauce. In Jewish cookery, meat stocks are traditionally made by simmering the coarser parts of root vegetables with herbs and koshered bones, enriched if desired with a piece of shin beef or a portion of fowl. To extract flavour from these ingredients, the stock must be simmered very slowly for many hours, preferably in the oven. However, with a pressure cooker, you can make excellent stock in just 1 hour. If stock is made the day before the soup, it should be chilled in the fridge – it will then be easy to lift off any fat on the surface. Stock is an excellent way of using up odds and ends of vegetables that have a good flavour but are too coarse to use in the soup itself. Here are some different ways to make meat stocks for soup. Each recipe makes approximately 1¼l/generous 2 pints of stock.

CHICKEN STOCK

Next time you roast or braise a chicken or fowl, freeze the cooked carcass and you will have the foundation for a low-fat chicken soup that can rival in flavour one enriched in the traditional way with a piece of fat hen.

To make the soup, break up the carcass so it will fit comfortably into the soup pan, stock pot or pressure cooker, add a couple of sets of giblets (omit the livers, as they impair the flavour), 2 fat carrots and the white part of a leek (both finely sliced), a few squashy tomatoes (or 2 teaspoons tomato purée), ½ large onion and a small bunch of parsley. Add 1.5l/2½ pints water, 1 teaspoon salt and 20 grinds of black pepper and allow the pot to simmer on the lowest possible heat for 3 hours (or pressure cook for 1 hour). Better still, simmer it in the oven, where it will develop an even richer flavour.

After this long, slow cooking, strain out the vegetables, bones and giblets, returning any chicken salvaged from them to the pan, then refrigerate or freeze overnight so that the fat content will solidify and can be easily removed next day. Or, pour off the fat in batches from the warm, strained stock using a large fat separator. When the soup is reheated, the chicken flavour will probably need strengthening with a couple of chicken stock cubes.

BEEF BONE STOCK

KEEPS FOR 3 DAYS IN THE FRIDGE | FREEZES FOR 3 MONTHS

500g/1lb 2oz koshered beef bones

fat leek, green part only

leaves from a head of celery

½ white turnip

½ onion

2 squashy tomatoes

1 bay leaf

20 peppercorns

1 large sprig of parsley

2 tsp salt

On the stove Put all the ingredients in a stock pot, bring to simmering point, then simmer on the top of the stove for 3 hours, or in the oven at 150°C/300°F/Gas 2 for the same length of time.

In a pressure cooker Put the bones and the coarsely cut vegetables into a pressure cooker and cover with cold water. Add the seasonings. Pressurize for 1 hour.

With either method, strain out all the vegetables. If the stock is not to be used at once, it can be either chilled until next day or boiled down to concentrate it, then poured into a plastic container and frozen.

BEEF AND BONE STOCK

Proceed as above, but add 225–450g/8oz–1 lb shin of beef to the vegetables. The cooked meat can be served in stock as a soup or used to fill pastries.

Note If a soup requires a long cooking time – for instance, barley soup and split-pea soup – the bones and meat (if using) can be cooked simultaneously with the soup ingredients. In that case, the bones should be put into the pan, covered with the amount of water specified in the recipe, and the mixture brought to the boil. The scum from the bones should then be carefully removed with a wet spoon before the cereals and vegetables are added.

ROAST BEEF BONE STOCK

The bone left from a roast rib of beef makes excellent stock. Proceed as above.

SOUP GARNISHES

KNAIDLACH MATZAH BALLS

SERVES 6–8

KEEPS FOR 2 DAYS IN THE FRIDGE | FREEZES FOR 1 MONTH

These are also sometimes called *halkes*. The secret of success is to use sufficient fat to make them tender yet still firm when the spoon goes in. Provided the specified amount of fat is used, the quantity of matzah meal may be increased if you prefer a firmer (though equally tender) texture.

2 large eggs

2 very slightly rounded tbsp rendered chicken fat, chicken-flavoured vegetable fat or soft margarine

100 ml/3½fl oz warm chicken soup, broth or water

1 tsp salt

¼ tsp white pepper

¼ tsp ground ginger

25g/1oz ground almonds

125g/4oz medium matzah meal

Whisk the eggs until fluffy, then stir in the soft fat, hand-hot soup or water, seasonings, ground almonds and matzah meal, and mix thoroughly. The mixture should look moist and thick, but should not be quite firm enough to form into balls. If too soft, add a little more meal; if too firm, add a teaspoon or two of water. Chill for at least an hour, but overnight will do no harm. The mixture will then firm up.

Half-fill a pan with water and bring to the boil, then add 2 teaspoons salt. Take pieces of the chilled mixture the size of large walnuts and roll between wetted palms into balls. Drop these balls into the boiling water, reduce the heat until the water is simmering, cover and simmer for 40 minutes without removing the lid. Strain from the water with a slotted spoon and drop into simmering soup.

For a small number or a special occasion, cook the knaidlach in chicken soup rather than in water. They will absorb some of the soup but with it also its delicious flavours.

Note To freeze knaidlach, open-freeze the cooked and drained knaidlach until solid – about 2 hours – then put them into plastic bags. To use, defrost for 1 hour at room temperature, then reheat in the simmering soup.

BAKED CROÛTONS
TO GARNISH MEAT SOUPS

SERVES 6–8
FREEZES FOR 3 MONTHS

4 large slices brown or rye bread

3 tbsp sunflower or olive oil

1 tsp dried Herbes de Provence

Preheat the oven to 180°C/350°F/Gas 4.

Cut the bread into 1 cm/½in cubes and mix in a flat baking tin with the oil and herbs. Bake in a moderate oven for 15–20 minutes, stirring once or twice so that the croûtons brown evenly.

BUTTERED CROÛTONS
TO GARNISH CREAM SOUPS

SERVES 4
LEFTOVERS FREEZE FOR 3 MONTHS

The garnish for a cream soup must be light yet crisp. Use slightly stale bread to get the crispiest results.

4 thin slices bread

25g/1oz/2 tbsp butter

1 tbsp oil

Cut the bread into 1 cm/½in cubes.

To fry Heat the butter and oil in a heavy frying pan. As soon as the foaming stops, put in the bread and fry gently until crisp and golden on all sides. Drain well on crumpled kitchen paper.

To bake Preheat oven to 180°C/350°F/Gas 4. Meanwhile, melt the butter and oil in a tray about 23 x 18cm/9 x 7in and 2.5cm/1 in deep. Add the croûtons, shake well to coat them with the fat, then bake for 15–20 minutes, shaking once, until crisp and golden brown. Drain on crumpled paper.

Reheat briefly in the oven just before serving in little pottery dishes.

SAUCES

TARTARE SAUCE

SERVES 4–6

KEEPS FOR 2 WEEKS IN THE FRIDGE | DO NOT FREEZE

A piquant sauce to serve with grilled, poached or fried fish such as lemon sole, haddock, plaice or halibut.

150ml/5fl oz mayonnaise

½ tbsp lemon juice

1 tbsp natural yogurt or fromage frais

1 small pickled cucumber, finely chopped

1 tsp snipped chives

1 tsp chopped tarragon

1 tsp chopped parsley

1 spring onion bulb or shallot, chopped

1 pinch of Cayenne pepper

3 stuffed olives, chopped

Mix all the ingredients together. Refrigerate for several hours to allow the flavours to blend.

EASY HOLLANDAISE SAUCE

SERVES 4
MAKE AND EAT ON THE SAME DAY

This way of making this delicious sauce is easy in comparison with the classic method! It is essential that both the liquids and the butter are thoroughly heated before they are added to the egg yolks.

1 tbsp lemon juice

½ tbsp white wine vinegar

125g/4½oz butter or margarine

2 egg yolks

½ tsp caster sugar

pinch of salt

Place the lemon juice and vinegar in a small saucepan and heat until bubbling. Heat the butter or margarine in another pan. In the blender or processor, blend the egg yolks, sugar and salt for 2 seconds. With the motor running, slowly trickle the vinegar mixture into the blender or food processor. Do the same with the foaming butter or margarine, slowly trickling it in until you have a thick, smooth sauce. Keep warm, if desired, in a heat-proof bowl standing in a pan of warm water.

VARIATIONS

SAUCE BÉARNAISE

Stir in 1½ tablespoons chopped tarragon or 1 teaspoon of dried tarragon after the butter or margarine has been added.

AVOCADO HOLLANDAISE

Peel 1 small, very ripe avocado and remove the pit. Purée the flesh in the food processor or blender, then remove. There is no need to wash the bowl. Make the sauce as above, then pulse or blend in the avocado purée.

DOUGHS, BATTERS AND PASTRY

KUCHEN DOUGH

MAKES I LARGE LOAF
KEEPS FOR 2 DAYS IN THE FRIDGE | UNRISEN DOUGH FREEZES FOR 3 MONTHS; SHAPED BUT UNBAKED
CAKES 2 WEEKS; BAKED CAKES 3 MONTHS

I egg

40ml/1¼fl oz/1½ tbsp cold milk

7g/¼oz/2 tsp easy-blend yeast, or
14g/½oz/¼ cake fresh yeast

225g/8oz plain white (all-purpose)
flour

½ tsp salt

40g/1½oz/3 tbsp soft butter or
margarine

grated zest of I lemon

40g/1½oz caster sugar

Break the egg into a measuring cup, add the cold milk, whisk to blend, then make up to 150ml/5fl oz with hot water. If you are using fresh yeast, add to the liquid and stir until dissolved. If you are using easy-blend yeast, put the flour, salt and sugar into the mixer bowl and mix thoroughly. Add the liquid, the soft butter and the lemon zest and beat for about 5 minutes until the dough is smooth and stretchy and leaves the bowl and the beater clean when pulled away. If too sticky, add a further 1–2 tablespoons of flour – the dough should be firm enough to form into a soft ball.

To rise and bake the same day Turn the dough on to a pastry board and knead for a few seconds – you will now have a satiny ball of dough. Grease a mixing bowl very lightly with oil, turn the ball of dough in it to coat it, then leave in the bowl and cover with cling film. It will take about 1½ hours in the kitchen to double in bulk. Then press the dough down, turn it over and knead it in the bowl for 1–2 minutes – this evenly distributes the gas bubbles in the dough.

To rise overnight Slip the dough into a greased plastic bag large enough to allow it to double in volume. Tie loosely and put on the bottom shelf of the fridge. Before using it next day, bring it out into the kitchen for 1 hour to return to room temperature. You can hasten the process by putting it in the microwave on defrost for 2 minutes. Knead for a further 1–2 minutes, as directed above.

In either case, leave the dough while you prepare the fillings.

QUICK KUCHEN BATTER

Quick kuchen is a general term to cover a wide range of cakes that can be topped either with sweet crumbles (usually called streusels) or with an assortment of seasonal fruits. These cakes do not have the same flavour or texture as a yeast-raised kuchen (see left), but they are still delicious

225g/8oz self-raising flour

1 tsp baking powder

75g/3oz/6 tbsp soft butter

125g/4oz caster sugar

1 large egg

150ml/5fl oz milk, or 125ml/4 fl oz if using a food processor

Put all the ingredients into a bowl and mix by hand or machine until a thick, smooth batter is formed – 15 seconds by food processor, 2–3 minutes by hand or electric mixer.

Oil either a rectangular cake tin measuring 30 x 23 x 5cm/12 x 9 x 2in or a 23cm/9in round or square tin of a similar depth. Spoon the batter into the chosen tin and level the top. The kuchen is now ready to be used.

CHEESECAKE PASTRY CRUST

**SUFFICIENT FOR A 23–25CM/9–10IN LOOSE-BOTTOMED FLAN TIN ABOUT 3CM/1¼IN DEEP OR AN 20CM/8IN TIN WITH SLOPING SIDES (MOULE À MANQUÉ) ABOUT 5CM/2IN DEEP
KEEPS IN THE FRIDGE FOR 2 DAYS | FREEZES FOR 3 MONTHS**

175g/6oz self-raising flour, plus extra for dusting

125g/4oz/8 tbsp butter or margarine

50g/2oz icing sugar

1 egg yolk (reserve the white for the filling, see traditional cheesecake, on page 146)

1 tbsp water

Put all the ingredients into a bowl and work together with a wooden spoon until a dough is formed. Chill for 30 minutes.

Roll out the pastry on a lightly floured board to fit the chosen tin, easing it in gently so as not to stretch it. Chill again while you prepare the filling.

ADAPTING RECIPES FOR THE KOSHER KITCHEN

Many recipes need adapting in some way before they can be used in the Jewish kitchen: they may contain non-kosher ingredients, or combine meat and dairy products in the same dish, or simply include a dairy food in a dish that is to be served as part of a meat meal. It is then a question of finding suitable alternative ingredients that, while satisfying the requirements of the dietary laws, will not radically alter the flavour and texture of the original dish. Here are suggestions for overcoming the common problems of five key ingredients.

Butter

- To fry meat and poultry – for each 2 tbsp butter, substitute 2 tbsp of olive or sunflower oil or a chicken-flavoured vegetable fat.
- To sauté vegetables for a meat casserole or soup – substitute an equal amount of margarine or olive oil.
- To fry or roast potatoes – for each 2 tbsp butter, substitute 2 tbsp of oil and scant 1 tbsp of margarine.
- In a sponge pudding or cake for a meat meal – substitute an equal amount of soft margarine; in addition, use water to mix instead of milk. If only a small number of eggs is included in the recipe, substitute an extra egg for 50ml/2fl oz of the milk.
- In pastry for a meat meal – for each 150g/5oz butter, substitute 125g/4oz margarine and 25g/1oz soft white fat (shortening).
- In the batter for dessert crêpes for a meat meal – substitute an equal amount of melted margarine (or sunflower oil for savoury crêpes).
- In a chicken stock for sauce – substitute an equal quantity of chicken-flavoured vegetable fat or soft margarine.
- To fry pancakes or crêpes for a meat meal – substitute a flavourless vegetable oil.
- To shallow-fry blintzes for a meat meal – substitute an equal quantity of margarine plus 1 tbsp flavourless (e.g. sunflower) oil to prevent over-browning of the margarine.

Milk

- In a batter for crêpes, blintzes, ordinary pancakes or Yorkshire pudding to serve at a meat meal – for each 275ml/10fl oz of milk, substitute 225ml/8fl oz of water plus 1 egg and 1 tbsp of flavourless oil. The blintzes and pancakes will be lighter and thinner, and fried stuffed blintzes will be crisper, than when made with milk. Yorkshire pudding will have a crisper crust, but a less spongy inside.
- In a sauce or soup that contains chicken or meat, or to serve at a meat meal – either substitute kosher non-dairy pouring cream or substitute chicken stock, making the soup look 'creamy' by whisking in 1 egg yolk for each 150ml/5fl oz of liquid and heat until steaming.

Cream

- To enrich a chicken sauce, soup or casserole – either substitute an equal quantity of unsweetened kosher non-dairy pouring cream (not whipping cream) or, for each 2–3 tbsp of cream, thicken the sauce with 1 egg yolk. Refrigerate for several hours to allow the cream to thicken.
- To substitute for whipped cream in a cold dessert – either for each 150ml/5fl oz of double or whipping cream substitute 125ml/4fl oz of kosher non-dairy whipping cream or, in a gelatine dessert, for every 150ml/5fl oz of double or whipping cream substitute a meringue made by whisking 2 egg whites until stiff and then whisking in 2 tsp of caster sugar – this will produce a lighter texture than cream.

Chicken Stock

- In a milk soup or sauce – substitute vegetable stock made with a cube or concentrate, or a chicken-flavoured parev stock cube or powder.

Shellfish

- In a fish cocktail or salad – substitute an equal weight of fillets of a firm white fish such as halibut, bream or lemon sole, poached, then cut into small cubes or coarsely flaked.
- In a creamed casserole or filling for pastry cases or fish pie – substitute an equal quantity of fresh salmon, halibut or haddock, poached, then flaked or cut in 2.5-cm/1-in cubes.
- In a deep-fried dish – substitute an equal weight of raw fillets of lemon sole, plaice or baby halibut, cut into bite-size strips. Coat with batter or with flour, egg and breadcrumbs and fry as directed.

INDEX

Thus sayeth Kohelet, 'There is nothing new under the sun', and of no sphere is this aphorism from Ecclesiastes more true than the world of food and cookery. My own knowledge is only the sum of that accumulated by hundreds of generations of Jewish women who have cooked before me. All I can hope to do is to make that knowledge relevant – and accessible – to people cooking at this particular time.

I must pay tribute to those women who cooked before me and who, without benefit of cookery books, established an oral tradition of superb Jewish food that has been passed down in an unbroken chain from mother to daughter – and not infrequently to son – from the beginning of our recorded history.

Evelyn Rose

PUBLISHER'S ACKNOWLEDGEMENTS

Each recipe in this book is the outcome not only of exhaustive research and recipe testing on the part of Evelyn Rose, but of the generations of Jewish cooks, past and present, who informed and inspired her work.

In particular the Publisher would like to thank Judi and David Rose for their support and advice.

All photography by Clare Winfield, prop stylist Wei Tang, and food stylist Jayne Cross.

First published in the United Kingdom in 2016 by
Pavilion
1 Gower Street
London
WC1E 6HD

ISBN 978-1-909108-72-1

A CIP catalogue record for this book is available from the British Library.

10 9 8 7 6 5 4 3 2 1

Reproduction by Colourdepth UK
Printed and bound by Toppan Printing International Ltd, China

This book can be ordered direct from the publisher at www.pavilionbooks.com

The recipes in this book were previously featured in **The New Complete International Jewish Cookbook** by Evelyn Rose (2011)